MADE TO REIGN

Using (And Losing) Your Kingly Authority

Loren VanGalder

All scripture quotations, unless otherwise indicated, are taken from the Holy Bible, New International Version®, NIV®. Copyright ©1973, 1978, 1984, 2011 by Biblica, Inc.™ All rights reserved worldwide. The "NIV" and "New International Version" are trademarks registered in the United States Patent and Trademark Office by Biblica, Inc.™

ISBN-10: 0989747204

ISBN-13: 978-0-989-7472-0-2

CONTENTS

Dedication

To the brothers in the church at the Federal Correctional Institution in Englewood, Colorado in 1993. You were the first I ever preached to about Saul.

To thousands of men I had the privilege of ministering to through my twenty-one years with the Federal Bureau of Prisons. I praise God for so many who are faithfully serving the Lord!

To my son Jeremiah. *"I know the plans I have for you,"* says the *Lord.* You were made to reign! Don't settle for less!

To all my spiritual sons. You're awesome!

Introduction

In the early nineties, while I was chaplain at the federal prison in Denver, there was a move of God among men. Many found healing, and strength to take their place at home and in society. Coach Bill McCartney had just started Promise Keepers, and I took some low custody inmates to one of their first rallies in Boulder. During those years I was impressed at how relevant King Saul's tragic life was for many men I was ministering to, and I preached a series of sermons from First Samuel which form the foundation of this book. The men's movement has died down, but that message is more urgent than ever. I've retired from prison chaplaincy and found that men on the street are just as hurting and broken as men in prison. The crisis in masculinity is evidenced by best sellers like *The End of Men.*

This is a book by a man, about men, and for men. Aside from a witch and fleeting references to his daughters, women are notably absent from King Saul's story. Maybe it would have a different ending if women were more involved. I believe God wants to lift you up as a man – but that in no way means putting down women. Godly authority and masculine strength – not abusive authority or weak men – allow women to flourish.

For many, the idea of men exercising kingly authority is quaint at best, but God is preparing his sons to reign with Christ. He made you to reign and wants you to use that authority instead of losing it, as Saul and so many men have.

PART ONE

Imagine God's excitement as he created Adam and commanded him: *"Rule, have dominion, over the fish in the sea and the birds in the sky and over every living creature that moves on the ground."*[1] He was given kingly authority, a garden paradise, and a gorgeous woman. Like Adam, you were created in the image of the King of the universe and given unlimited potential as his adopted son. God designed you to be the head, with authority in your home and community. You were made to reign, but usually there are some hard lessons on the way to the throne.

A man's journey through life can be described in various ways, but there are some fairly obvious stages. First is spring, if you're thinking of your life as seasons of the year. If it's a day, this is morning. It's a time of preparation and formation, where you learn to hear and respond to God's voice. As a young man you have great vision and energy, but you're still trying to figure out what it means to be a man. It's normal to wrestle with insecurity. You want things to happen faster - but take your time. You're laying the foundation for the rest of your life.

If you're on this first part of the journey I want to walk with you and encourage you. I don't want you to repeat others' mistakes and miss out on the fullness of what God has for you. New responsibilities can seem overwhelming. There's so much to do. It's easy to neglect the most important things, like God and family. Develop healthy spiritual disciplines. Eat right and exercise. Get to know your wife and learn how to love her. I've seen too many young men with beautiful wives oblivious to this treasure God's given them - too caught up in their career, having fun, and figuring themselves out. Pay attention to warning signs and do something about them, or later on they'll make you miserable. Above all, enjoy God and all he's given you! It may not seem like it, but this is a great time with tremendous possibilities! It's time for you to begin to reign!

If you're further along the journey, young men are in desperate need of older men to guide them and walk with them. Studying Saul may show you what went right or wrong in your life, so you can wisely use your kingly authority now and help others avoid your mistakes.

Chapter 1

Israel Requests a King:
1 Samuel 8:1-20

God seems to have a problem finding men who will faithfully exercise kingly authority. Adam certainly didn't, and we're still paying for it. Much later, Moses brought God's people out of slavery in Egypt and Joshua led them in conquering the promised land. When he died, the nation slid into chaos. The last verse of Judges says: *In those days Israel had no king; everyone did as he saw fit.* But they did have a king - Israel was a theocracy, and God was their king. Since they weren't acknowledging his lordship or obeying his laws, he raised up an assortment of "judges" to provide leadership. You may have heard of Gideon's fleece, and Samson's great strength and betrayal by Delilah.[2] There was no capital or temple, so the tent Moses made on the wilderness journey from Egypt was still the center of worship and government.

As First Samuel begins, Eli, the tabernacle priest, was the nation's leader. Apparently he was not the best father, if you can judge a man by his sons. They were among the most evil in the land. There was no way God would allow them to rule, although he did use Eli as a mentor and spiritual father to the next leader, a young prophet named Samuel. He'd been a miracle baby, born to a barren woman, given to the Lord in keeping with a vow she'd made, and raised by Eli.[3] God spoke through Samuel and

5

helped him lead the nation to victory against the ever-threatening Philistines. It's probably not coincidence that Samuel, like his mentor, had problems with his sons. It's his only real fault. God kept looking for a man to provide a line of rulers, but neither Eli nor Samuel was it.[4] It would only be his own Son, of the line of David, who would establish that lasting kingdom. But for now, Israel's had enough of Samuel's family problems.

When Samuel grew old, he appointed his sons as Israel's leaders. The name of his firstborn was Joel and the name of his second was Abijah, and they served at Beersheba. But his sons did not follow his ways. They turned aside after dishonest gain and accepted bribes and perverted justice. So all the elders of Israel gathered together and came to Samuel at Ramah. They said to him, "You are old, and your sons do not follow your ways; now appoint a king to lead us, such as all the other nations have." (1-3)

Samuel should have taken the initiative in seeking God's will for the nation's future, but he couldn't admit his sons were unfit to rule. It's easy to ignore family problems - until your wife leaves, your daughter turns up pregnant, or your son lands in jail. Without godly leadership, people naturally follow the world. All the other nations had kings, so that's what Israel wanted. The only problem was they weren't like other nations. Trying to be like the world is asking for trouble. Samuel knew that, and he decides to pray about it.

But when they said, "Give us a king to lead us," this displeased Samuel; so he prayed to the Lord.

And the Lord told him: "Listen to all that the people are saying to you; it is not you they have rejected, but they have rejected me as their king. As they have done from the day I brought them up out of Egypt until this day, forsaking me and serving other gods, so they are doing to you. Now listen to them; but warn them solemnly and let them know what the king who will reign over them will claim as his rights." (6-9)

Wouldn't it be great to get an immediate, verbal, response to your prayers, even if it's not what you want to hear?

Rejection

God didn't want Samuel's sons to lead the nation, and Israel didn't want him or his sons. Samuel feels rejected, but God quickly pulls him out of his self-pity: "It's not about you, Samuel!" Rejection hurts, but they're really rejecting God, and he's used to it. He's experienced more rejection than you ever will, for no reason. He'd fought their battles and faithfully led them without a single mistake, but Israel didn't want him to lead them or fight for them. They wanted a man, a king, to lead them. They wanted to fight their own battles.

A godly leader often bears the brunt of peoples' anger, disappointment, and struggles with God. It's a lot easier to blame a man than blame God, or admit they're rejecting him. Don't be surprised if you experience the same rejection and rebellion. If you've been rejected, by your church or by your wife, try not to take it personally. Let God deal with it. Draw close to him in your pain, and leave your self-pity there. He understands. Let him strengthen you.

The cost of doing it your way

When you feel rejected, it's easy to act out of hurt and anger. If you're in power, you may force your will on others and purposely withhold what they want. Men often do that with their wives or children. Maybe your dad, or a boss, has done it. Maybe you have. Not God. He wasn't happy, but he'll let them have their king. There may be times you insist on something – and God lets you have it, even if he intended something better. God gives you responsibility and the room to fail. Your prayers can move God, even in a direction he might prefer not to go. It's part of teaching you how to reign. God redeemed their blunder and used kings for the good of the nation, but there are always consequences of rejecting him and doing things your own way. Samuel was only too happy to tell the people the trouble a king would bring, probably hoping they'd see the light and withdraw their request.

Samuel told all the words of the Lord to the people who were asking him for a king. He said, "This is what the king who will reign over you will claim as his rights: He will take your sons and make them serve with his chariots and horses, and they will run in front of his chariots. Some he will assign to be commanders of thousands and commanders of fifties, and others to plow his ground and reap his harvest, and still others to make weapons of war and equipment for his chariots. He will take your daughters to be perfumers and cooks and bakers. He will take the best of your fields and vineyards and olive groves and give them to his attendants. He will take a tenth of your grain and of your vintage and give it to his officials and attendants. Your male and female servants and the best of your cattle and donkeys he will take for his own use. He will take a tenth of your flocks, and you yourselves will become his slaves. When that day comes, you will cry out for relief from the king you have chosen, but the Lord will not answer you in that day." (10-18)

Wouldn't that make you think twice? You'd expect the people to wake up, fall before God in repentance, and beg him to be their king, but the warning fell on deaf ears. Have you stubbornly insisted on doing things your way, even after being warned by a pastor, friend, or family member? Is there a warning you need to listen to right now?

Perhaps most sobering, God will turn a deaf ear when they cry out for relief. At times God says he will *not* answer prayer - at least the way we hope he will. *"When I called, they did not listen; so when they called, I would not listen," says the Lord Almighty.*[5]

You may have to live with the answers to your prayers. God may not give you another job after you begged for the promotion that's causing you so much stress. You have to stay with the wife you so earnestly asked for. If you're wondering why God doesn't seem to be answering your prayers, examine where your heart's at, and whether you're experiencing the consequences of a past decision.

But the people refused to listen to Samuel. "No!" they said. "We want a king over us. Then we will be like all the other nations, with a king to lead us and to go out before us and fight our battles." (19-20)

Who wants to be different? Israel wasn't sure they wanted to be a holy people, set apart for God, a "peculiar" people, as the King James translated it. We want to be accepted and seen as normal, so we run after all the world offers, even if we do "Christianize" it.

Samuel still thought hearing the consequences would change their minds. It doesn't, so all he can do is go back to God. *When Samuel heard all that the people said, he repeated it before the Lord.* (21) As though the Lord hadn't heard them! *The Lord answered, "Listen to them and give them a king." Then Samuel said to the Israelites, "Everyone go back to your own town." (22)* If they're determined to have a king, they'll get a king. Samuel can only wait for God to show him what to do next. At least the people obeyed him and didn't insist on naming their own king right then. They're not in a good place spiritually, and have high expectations of a king. How would you feel as a farm boy being told you're going to be that king? Even an experienced, godly man would find it challenging.

Is God truly your King? Or are you fighting your own battles? Are you pushing ahead with worldly success that may just cause you problems? Have you been asking God for something - so you can be like everyone else? In the process, are you rejecting God's plan for you?

Chapter 2

God Calls Saul:
1 Samuel 9:1-21

Introducing: Saul

There's a look the media calls "presidential." You rarely see someone running for top office who's short, overweight, or unattractive. First impressions mean a lot. Saul was *"without equal among the Israelites."*[6] Even the Bible compares him with other men. We do that all the time, don't we? Often it's subconscious. If we measure up well, we feel good. If we don't, we feel insecure, or envy their good looks and favor with God. You may not look presidential, but that's okay. Give up the comparison game. Accept yourself as God made you and accept others as they are. You'll find it very liberating.

There was a Benjamite, a man of standing, whose name was Kish son of Abiel, the son of Zeror, the son of Bekorath, the son of Aphiah of Benjamin. Kish had a son named Saul, as handsome a young man as could be found anywhere in Israel, and he was a head taller than anyone else. (1-2)

Saul was tall and handsome, which conveyed authority. He came from a wealthy family with a highly respected father. Ancestry is important to God, and Saul had good roots. What do you know about your great-great grandfathers? Or your spiritual heritage? A curse placed on your grandfather could be passed down to you. Study your family background to see how it impacts you today.

God apparently saw something in Saul. He chose him out of all the men in Israel, although as we study his life we may wonder why. What kind of people do you choose as friends? We often don't understand what draws us to certain people, but pay attention; God may have a purpose in it.

Unfortunately, handsome men from great backgrounds with high IQs and good education are not guaranteed success. Today we know the importance of the "EQ" - emotional quotient. A leader needs to relate well to people, whether in government, business, or the church. We have no idea what Saul's IQ was, but we'll find his EQ seems low.

Saul's job preparation

Saul had a good background, but was he ready to reign? When you meet a man he'll typically ask what you *do*, while God is more concerned with whom you *are*. Saul was a farmer and shepherd, and wasn't doing anything too impressive when God called him to be king.

Now the donkeys belonging to Saul's father Kish were lost, and Kish said to his son Saul, "Take one of the servants with you and go and look for the donkeys." So he passed through the hill country of Ephraim and through the area around Shalisha, but they did not find them. They went on into the district of Shaalim, but the donkeys were not there. Then he passed through the territory of Benjamin, but they did not find them. (3-5)

Was this the most important thing he'd ever done? His father entrusted him with rounding up lost donkeys, but he never even found them! Little did he realize this insignificant task would lead him to a life-changing encounter with God. Don't look down on humble chores or feel bad about apparent failure. You never know what God has planned!

But the servant replied, "Look, in this town there is a man of God; he is highly respected, and everything he says comes true. Let's go there now. Perhaps he will tell us what way to take."

Saul said to his servant, "If we go, what can we give the man? The food in our sacks is gone. We have no gift to take to the man of God. What do we have?"

The servant answered him again. "Look," he said, "I have a quarter of a shekel of silver. I will give it to the man of God so that he will tell us what way to take." (Formerly in Israel, if someone went to inquire of God, they would say, "Come, let us go to the seer," because the prophet of today used to be called a seer.)

"Good," Saul said to his servant. "Come, let's go." So they set out for the town where the man of God was. (6-10)

Saul obviously wasn't into politics. He didn't know who Samuel was, even though he'd been leading the nation for years and was probably the best-known man in Israel. Nor is his spirituality impressive - his servant had to suggest seeking God's help. Even here Saul is more concerned with appearances, like having a gift for the prophet.

As they were going up the hill to the town, they met some young women coming out to draw water, and they asked them, "Is the seer here?"

"He is," they answered. "He's ahead of you. Hurry now; he has just come to our town today, for the people have a sacrifice at the high place. As soon as you enter the town, you will find him before he goes up to the high place to eat. The people will not begin eating until he comes, because he must bless the sacrifice; afterward, those who are invited will eat. Go up now; you should find him about this time." (11-12)

On the outskirts of town, the well was hard to miss, and weary, thirsty, travelers would stop there first.[7] If you want God to use you, go where the people are.

They went up to the town, and as they were entering it, there was Samuel, coming toward them on his way up to the high place.

Now the day before Saul came, the Lord had revealed this to Samuel: "About this time tomorrow I will send you a man from the land of Benjamin. Anoint him ruler over my people Israel; he will deliver them from the hand of the Philistines. I have looked on my people, for their cry has reached me."

When Samuel caught sight of Saul, the Lord said to him, "This is the man I spoke to you about; he will govern my people." (13-17)

Even as a child Samuel had enjoyed an intimate relationship with God and the privilege of hearing his audible voice. He was that rare man the Lord could count on to do his work. God had already talked with him, and now he just "happened" to meet Saul on his way to the high place. When you're walking with the Lord there are no coincidences. God's in control, and if he has a purpose to accomplish, he'll put all the pieces in place. God arranged the lost donkeys to get Saul out of his house. Some would say his failure to find them was due to sin or lack of faith, but it caused him to look for Samuel. Pay attention to what's going on around you. Be alert to those people you just "happen" to meet. If you're available to God, he'll show you what to do and give you some great opportunities to minister. What might he have for you today?

Saul's new calling

Saul approached Samuel in the gateway and asked, "Would you please tell me where the seer's house is?"

"I am the seer," Samuel replied. "Go up ahead of me to the high place, for today you are to eat with me, and in the morning I will send you on your way and will tell you all that is in your heart. As for the donkeys you lost three days ago, do not worry about them; they have been found. And to whom is all the desire of Israel turned, if not to you and your whole family line?" (18-20)

Samuel's conveniently in the gateway. He assures Saul that lost donkeys are no problem for God. We get anxious about lost donkeys when God is preparing us for much greater things! God has bigger plans for Saul than rescuing donkeys. The next morning Samuel would tell Saul everything in his heart! What would Saul think learning that all the desire of Israel was turned to him and his family? How would you respond hearing you're going to be king? How do you feel about God choosing you to reign with Christ? God knows you as intimately as he knew Saul. He can reveal what's in your heart through a word of knowledge, just as he can give you that insight into someone else. Show the same interest for them that Samuel did for Saul. Be sensitive to their concern for lost donkeys. Sit down to share a meal, and spend time with them.

Saul answered, "But am I not a Benjamite, from the smallest tribe of Israel, and is not my clan the least of all the clans of the tribe of Benjamin? Why do you say such a thing to me?" (21)

God loves to go against what the world values and often chooses to use what appears poor, weak, and despised - but Saul didn't know that. Benjamin was the last of Jacob's sons, and the tribe had shrunk during the time of the judges.[8] God had chosen an insignificant family from the smallest tribe, which didn't make sense to Saul. Surely God would choose someone from a prominent family in a major tribe - like Judah. How could he choose you?

God has chosen you and called you

God chose Israel, and from that nation called a few people as leaders. There's something about being chosen by God which profoundly impacts our identity. It enabled the Jews to survive the horrors of exile and dispersion. Today, Jesus is choosing many and *has made [them] to be a kingdom and priests to serve his God and Father.*[9] God's chosen you to be adopted as his son, holy and blameless in his sight. Knowing that should shape your identity and make you feel very special - and humbled. If you've ever questioned whether you're one of the chosen, be assured that God has chosen you. It's not by accident you're reading this. Just as God arranged the circumstances in Saul's life, he arranged for you to get this book. If you've never received a call from God, he's calling you right now. The call is simply to follow Jesus. Once he calls, you can't go on with life as usual. He won't force you one way or the other, but you have to tell him yes or no. Have you responded to that call? You can begin a new life right now, simply by asking God to forgive you and deciding to follow Jesus.

If you're following Jesus, you're in his kingdom, and everyone in the kingdom has a job. When he calls you to do something, you don't have the luxury of refusing. Remember that it's God calling. He's not looking for volunteers. There was no search committee to interview candidates for king. No ads were put in newspapers, no message sent out on Facebook or Twitter. Saul didn't get a chance to review the job description and decide if he wanted to be king or not. Had Saul refused God's call he wouldn't have been thrown out of Israel, but his life would have been rough. If you run from your calling you won't lose your salvation, but you'll be very frustrated. Maybe Saul had hoped to have his own herd of goats someday, but now all that's changed. Every young man wants to make an impact on his world, but suddenly he's pulled into something much bigger than he ever imagined. His self-image and relationship with God were weak, so he didn't believe God could use him. But as surely as God found his lost donkeys, he can be confident God Almighty will be with him to accomplish all he's been chosen for. He was made to reign, and so are you.

God choosing you is every bit as amazing as him choosing a young farm boy from the least tribe of Israel to be king. And you're chosen for something far greater than directing the affairs of a tiny nation. You may not agree with God's choice and wonder why he would choose you. He called many people in the Bible who felt they weren't qualified. Your natural abilities don't determine what God can do with your life. He can make up for any deficiencies. In fact, it's harder for him to work with someone who's overly confident. He's chosen you because he loves you and has a purpose for you. In your calling you'll find fulfillment. Are you shocked that the God of the universe would use you to do mighty things? Do you put limits on him? Do you have any business questioning whom God chooses to do his work? Do you know your calling? If not, get in a place where you can hear God, where a man of God can speak into your life. If you know your calling, what are you doing with it? Trials will surely come, you'll question it, and you may have to wait to see it fulfilled, but the knowledge that God has called you should help you to persevere.

God designed you for more than chasing lost donkeys. You were made to reign. Your life is about to change. Dramatically.

When You Call My Name[10]

There's a hunger in this wilderness for your revelation
To hear the words of life that strengthen me
Come and show what you've prepared for me speak your
confirmation
Show me how I fit into your plan

For when you call my name I can see again
Who you are and who I'm meant to be
And as you beckon me I am free to see
Who you are and who I'm sent to be

I am seeking true identity in the light of your presence
I am longing to know how you see me
In the time that you have given me, release the strength to follow
And the grace to be who you say I am

Chapter 3

Ready to Reign:
1 Samuel 9:22-10:13

Saul started the day looking for donkeys. By evening he was dining with the most important man in Israel. God often works subtly and slowly, but when it's time, things can change fast, and dramatically.[11] Remember how Joseph's brothers sold him into slavery in Egypt? He spent years in preparation, but within a day he moved from prison to the palace. It may seem slow in coming, but at the right time God will reveal his amazing plans and provision. Are you ready? He has something special planned, set aside, and kept - just for you.

Then Samuel brought Saul and his servant into the hall and seated them at the head of those who were invited—about thirty in number. Samuel said to the cook, "Bring the piece of meat I gave you, the one I told you to lay aside."

So the cook took up the thigh with what was on it and set it in front of Saul. Samuel said, "Here is what has been kept for you. Eat, because it was set aside for you for this occasion from the time I said, 'I have invited guests.'" And Saul dined with Samuel that day. (9:22-24)

What a dinner! Samuel goes all out to give Saul a taste of what God's prepared for him. Saul doesn't know it, but he just got a spiritual father. A good mentoring relationship is invaluable, whether it's formally established or not.[12] You may be mentoring someone now without knowing it. Eli had mentored Samuel, and now Samuel naturally steps into that role with Saul.[13] Unfortunately, like many busy Christian leaders, Eli and Samuel were not great fathers to their own sons. You learn how to be a man and a father from your dad, but if that didn't happen, God may give you a spiritual father.

After they came down from the high place to the town, Samuel talked with Saul on the roof of his house. They rose about daybreak, and Samuel called to Saul on the roof, "Get ready, and I will send you on your way." When Saul got ready, he and Samuel went outside together. As they were going down to the edge of the town, Samuel said to Saul, "Tell the servant to go on ahead of us"—and the servant did so—"but you stay here for a while, so that I may give you a message from God." (9:25-27)

A spiritual father brings his son into godly company

Simply being together was more important than what was said or done. Something powerful happened in Saul at the high place, at the head of the dinner table, and up on the roof. How often did boys get invited to the roof to talk with grown men? When Saul was ready to leave, Samuel didn't just show him the door. He went with him to the edge of town. Samuel was walking with Saul, building confidence in the young ruler, as God began to transform him from a nobody into a king.

Has anyone taken you along as they served God? Do you long for a father or older man to pull you aside, to sit and talk with you? If you've had that privilege, thank God, and consider yourself fortunate. If not, ask God to bring someone into your life, and don't be afraid to ask that man if you can spend time with him.

Do you look for younger men God is touching - and reach out to them? Do you take the opportunity to give them a place of honor in the gathering of men? As you look for younger men to mentor, be sure not to overlook your own son. It could change his life – and yours.

Unfortunately, there's a word of caution here. Too often an older man has singled out a young man with less than honorable intentions. If God has entrusted you with someone, you have an awesome responsibility before the Lord to maintain total purity in that relationship, and I'm not just talking about sexual sin. There are other ways we can abuse young men and use them for our own purposes. Keep a check on your heart and maintain accountability with others, avoiding anything that could look suspicious.

If you've been abused by a Christian mentor, or anyone else, God wants to heal those deep wounds, restore trust, and bring truly godly men into your life. But be careful of blindly trusting others – that perfect father-figure you so long for probably doesn't exist.

A spiritual father brings a word from the Lord

Companionship and a good example are important, but there was something more Saul needed - a word from God. It can be Scripture, or a word God places in your heart. Not that you must have a profound, prophetic word every time you get together. Pray over it, and when you have a word, be faithful to share it. Don't hold back because you feel awkward about it, or are afraid of offending him and losing his friendship. If you earn the right to speak into his life he'll eagerly receive any word. This is a big responsibility! Don't take it lightly! If a mentor speaks into your life, listen carefully, write it down, and pray about it. Those words are valuable. If you've never gotten a word from your spiritual father, ask him to pray about receiving a word from God for you. He may not be used to speaking into someone's life. Assure him you'd love to hear whatever God might give him.

Samuel's word for Saul

Then Samuel took a flask of olive oil and poured it on Saul's head and kissed him, saying, "Has not the Lord anointed you ruler over his inheritance? When you leave me today, you will meet two men near Rachel's tomb, at Zelzah on the border of Benjamin. They will say to you, 'The donkeys you set out to look for have been found. And now your father has stopped thinking about them and is worried about you. He is asking, "What shall I do about my son?"' Then you will go on from there until you reach the great tree of Tabor. Three men going up to worship God at Bethel will meet you there. One will be carrying three young goats, another three loaves of bread, and another a skin of wine. They will greet you and offer you two loaves of bread, which you will accept from them.

"After that you will go to Gibeah of God, where there is a Philistine outpost. As you approach the town, you will meet a procession of prophets coming down from the high place with lyres, timbrels, pipes and harps being played before them, and they will be prophesying. The Spirit of the Lord will come powerfully upon you, and you will prophesy with them; and you will be changed into a different person. Once these signs are fulfilled, do whatever your hand finds to do, for God is with you.

"Go down ahead of me to Gilgal. I will surely come down to you to sacrifice burnt offerings and fellowship offerings, but you must wait seven days until I come to you and tell you what you are to do." (10:1-8)

Talk about detailed instructions! After the events of the last couple days, how would you feel as a young man hearing this? God knows your heart and your future, just like he knew Saul's. Can you think of anyone better to guide you? Most men are serious about running (or ruining) their own lives – and they do. Placing your life in God's hands and trusting him to handle the details frees you up to hear about your future.

Before the word comes the anointing, the symbol of the Holy Spirit, which usually was reserved for priests. God is equipping his first king. The word without the Spirit can be rigid and overwhelming; the Spirit without the word can lead to all kinds of excess. We need both. As a spiritual father, keep that balance, and be open to prophetic symbols such as anointing with oil or foot washing.

Saul's told in great detail what will happen, probably to test his obedience and assure him this really was the Lord. After all, he could have decided the whole thing was crazy and just gone home. Saul will end up joining this amazing procession. We don't know much about these "schools" of prophets God called together for ministry and encouragement. This group had been to the mountain top, offering sacrifices at the high place, and they're in the Spirit, playing instruments, prophesying, and praising God. We usually think of prophecy as proclaiming a message from God, but this prophecy seems to be anointed, perhaps ecstatic, praise. Numbers records the same phenomena when the Spirit rested on the seventy elders.[14] The disciples' experience on Pentecost was not totally new to the Jews. Like the Upper Room in the second chapter of Acts, this is an atmosphere in which Saul can readily receive the Spirit.

Results of the Spirit's coming

Saul had already been chosen and anointed, but this outpouring of the Spirit gave him the power he needed. Christ's disciples were to wait in Jerusalem until they received that power. Christians differ on the semantics and exact process - but we need that power. I'm more concerned with a life that reflects the power of the Spirit than *when* or *how* you receive him. Just because Saul received the Spirit this way doesn't mean anyone else will. We're too quick to organize our version of a "prophetic procession," playing the same music, and trying to make people receive the Spirit a certain way. However it happens, God wants you to experience the Spirit's fullness. Have you?

Joining with others to worship God

Once the Spirit came, Saul would join others walking in the Spirit and be drawn to worship and praise God, just as in Numbers and at Pentecost. Now the Lord can shape him as a man of God and part of a community of prophets. Saul became so identified with them that a saying arose: "Is Saul among the prophets?" Wouldn't it be great to be identified with men of God like that? Had Saul held onto it and nurtured it, his life might have turned out differently.

Those relationships and that heartfelt worship were intended to form the foundation of his reign. Unfortunately, he waited years, until he was tormented by evil spirits, to get back into worship. By then it was so foreign he had to rely on David to worship God and bring him some relief. Worship is powerful. What part does it play in your life? I'm not just talking about listening to worship music or going to a church known for its great worship band. "Worship" services seem to increasingly be performances where few are really worshiping God. Jesus said the Father seeks those who worship him in spirit and truth.[15] The Spirit of God will help you become a true worshiper.

Changed into another man

Saul himself said his qualifications weren't too impressive, but God simply changed him into another man. Your problems and limitations aren't that important. When you come to Christ, God isn't interested in rehabilitating or improving you. He just makes you a new man. The change is so dramatic Jesus called it being "born again." The apostle Peter is a great example of the change the Spirit brings. He cowardly denied knowing Christ, but when the Spirit came on him at Pentecost, he was changed, and got up to boldly preach the Gospel to thousands.[16]

If you're truly born again, there should be a noticeable change in your life. Are you a "new creation?" Are you born again? Would you say you've been changed into a different person, or are there only glimpses of the Spirit's presence and power in a fleshly, worldly, life? Are you still struggling in your own strength to bring about change little by little? It's wonderful to experience the initial fullness of the Holy Spirit, but for a transformed life you must walk daily in his power. You can quench, grieve, or ignore him. God did his part in totally changing Saul, but Saul still has to foster that relationship and continue to allow the Spirit freedom in his life. Unfortunately, he didn't.

Do whatever your hand finds to do

Samuel concludes with an amazing promise: *"Once these signs are fulfilled, do whatever your hand finds to do, for God is with you."* God gave a similar promise to Joshua, if he would be bold and live his life in obedience to the Word of God.[17] He's not guaranteed success, at least in our understanding of it, but it's implied that God's blessing will be on whatever he does.

Wouldn't you love to have that kind of guarantee? I believe you can. Get into Scripture to learn God's heart, and then walk in his ways. He wants to bless and use you, and he will, as you are filled, motivated, and directed by the Spirit. Many men feverishly seek God's will, yet spend frustrated lives feeling they're accomplishing nothing. Saul didn't have to try and figure out what God wanted. If he was walking in the Spirit he could go ahead and do whatever his hand found to do, because God was with him. If you're living in the power of the Spirit and under Christ's Lordship, God is with you! He's allowing the situations and opportunities that come into your life. Look at how he sovereignly arranged things for Saul! He certainly can do the same for you! You may just need to get moving - or you may need to wait.

Wait

All this would happen only *"once these signs are fulfilled."* Samuel's final instruction hints at what eventually causes Saul's downfall. He had to wait. Wait for Samuel, and wait for God's timing. If Saul is to succeed as king, he must have patience to wait and be obedient to instructions that may not make sense to him. An arrogant young man might feel he has no further need of an old prophet, but God's letting him know Samuel will continue to play an important role in his life. Part of mentoring is sending the young man on ahead. You don't want to smother him, but he also needs to be confident you'll come through on your word. If you say you're going to meet him at a certain time, or join him to do something, make sure you do!

Have these signs been fulfilled in your life? Many don't wait to become part of a company of Spirit-filled believers, enter into worship, or be changed. They push ahead in the flesh and wonder why everything falls apart. If the disciples had tried to organize a mass crusade before Pentecost, it would have been a disaster. Are you willing to wait for God's time, and trust him with the details?

As Saul turned to leave Samuel, God changed Saul's heart, and all these signs were fulfilled that day. When he and his servant arrived at Gibeah, a procession of prophets met him; the Spirit of God came powerfully upon him, and he joined in their prophesying. When all those who had formerly known him saw him prophesying with the prophets, they asked each other, "What is this that has happened to the son of Kish? Is Saul also among the prophets?"

After Saul stopped prophesying, he went to the high place. (10:9-13)

Trust God's word! God faithfully did exactly what he said he would. As Saul turned to leave, God changed his heart. Hopefully you've had times living in the power of the Spirit when God blessed everything you did. You may also know what it's like to have everything fail if you fall back into walking in the flesh, although sometimes we're so out of touch with God we don't even stop to realize that something's seriously wrong.

You may hold back from fully serving God because you feel inadequate or have too many problems. God has a purpose for your life and can completely change you, just like he changed Saul. He may be setting up your circumstances, as he did for Saul. Reading this book might even be part of it! God arranged for Saul to meet Spirit-filled prophets; he may arrange for you to meet a Spirit-filled man as well. You too may freely join in praise and worship and become a totally different man.

You may be about Saul's age. Your heart's longing to serve God and make a difference for him, but your passions can go wild and get you into all kinds of trouble. Often the response is to bridle them, but God gave you those passions – and he wants to direct them in a way that will glorify him, and benefit you and the world. He wants to use your life! Worship and relationships to other godly men are part of it, but you can't experience God's purpose until the Spirit comes on you. Has he filled your life? You'll know when he does. Once that's settled, the word of God may be *"do whatever your hand finds to do, for God is with you."*

If you're an older man you may remember being excited about what could happen in your life, but through the years and many disappointments you've become cynical and lost that passion. When you see a young man like Saul, you feel a little awe - and even envy. You may feel your heart stirred again with what God wanted to do with your manhood. Share your wisdom with a Saul, while renewing your passion for Jesus, your family, and God's work in the world.

Chapter 4

Hiding in the Baggage:
1 Samuel 10:14-27

When Saul woke up the morning after visiting the high place, it probably all seemed like a dream. A couple days before he was an unknown shepherd looking for lost donkeys. Then he meets the most powerful man in Israel and finds out he'll be king. A supernatural encounter with God is great, but what happens next? You come home full of the Spirit, anxious to share it with your wife - and get into a fight. It seems like you left the Spirit in church. You're right back in the flesh. The morning after that heavy time at the altar it just doesn't feel so real. Has anything changed? Was it just emotion? Maybe God spoke to you in the first few chapters of this book, but now you're not so sure about it. There's nothing wrong with you. It's hard coming down from the mountain top.

Back Home

Saul was given a word from God. Every detail was perfectly fulfilled. What was he supposed to do now? Find a throne somewhere and issue a press release that he's the new king? That wouldn't work, would it? Yet I've seen all too many men try to make their calling happen on their own. You usually don't start on the throne. God brings it about in his way and his time. Typically there'll be lots of hard lessons along the way. Be alert to open doors and people he brings into your life. The lessons often start with your own family.

Saul headed home to get on with his life, almost like nothing happened. Picture him walking into his house (or tent, as it may be): "Hey Uncle, how you doing? I'm good. I'm not the same person I was when I left here last week. God changed me. By the way, I'm gonna be your king." How do you break that news? After a special encounter with God it can be tough going home. Thank God for the families who rejoice and encourage you, but often they're skeptical. They know you.

Saul was given the perfect opening: *Now Saul's uncle asked him and his servant, "Where have you been?"* (14) Chances are by this point Saul didn't feel God's presence as he had with the prophets. His servant didn't say a word, although you have to wonder what he might have shared with the other servants. Instead of affirming in faith what God had done, Saul chose to hide it:

"Looking for the donkeys," he said. "But when we saw they were not to be found, we went to Samuel."

Saul's uncle said, "Tell me what Samuel said to you."

Another opening, and another missed opportunity:

Saul replied, "He assured us that the donkeys had been found." But he did not tell his uncle what Samuel had said about the kingship. (15-16)

Some have suggested that Saul was told not to mention the kingship - but he could have shared about his encounter with God. Read Scripture carefully. There's a purpose in the words used. God's telling us Saul passed up an important chance to speak. He didn't lie, but he told half-truths - leaving out the most important details. Saul seems to be acting on his feelings instead of God's promises. God already said he was with Saul, but Saul was acting as if that wasn't true. He was to do whatever he found to do, and the first thing he was given to do was share what God had done. Not that hard, right? But we're often afraid to open our mouths. His uncle gave him two perfect opportunities, and God will do the same for you. It's important to talk about *all* God has done in your life. Don't hide it. When they notice a change in you, be honest about what Jesus has done. If you were in church last night and someone asks what you did, don't just say "I hung out with some friends." You're not lying, but you're telling half-truths, and quenching the Spirit.

The Holy Spirit dramatically came on Saul, but now those feelings are gone. If you've asked God to fill you with his Spirit, don't rely on your feelings. You can stand on two simple truths: God says you *need* his Spirit and he *wants* to fill you.[18] Paul says we receive the Spirit just as we receive Jesus – by faith.[19] Unless you're full of sin or doubt, you can be confident God *has* filled you if you asked in faith.

The Public Selection of a King

Maybe Saul hoped Samuel would forget the whole thing. It would be easier to go back to tending donkeys. It might be easier for you to forget about God's call on your life and hope the pastor who spoke over you forgets about it too, but thank God for faithful men true to his word who won't let us back out of his calling. Samuel set up an elaborate process to choose the king, giving every tribe a chance, so it would be clear that God chose Saul.

Samuel summoned the people of Israel to the Lord at Mizpah and said to them, "This is what the Lord, the God of Israel, says: 'I brought Israel up out of Egypt, and I delivered you from the power of Egypt and all the kingdoms that oppressed you.' But you have now rejected your God, who saves you out of all your disasters and calamities. And you have said, 'No, appoint a king over us.' So now present yourselves before the Lord by your tribes and clans." (17-19)

God seems to give the nation one last chance to repent of rejecting him, but they're determined to get their king. What happened next would be comical if it wasn't so sad.

Hiding in the Baggage

When Samuel had all Israel come forward by tribes, the tribe of Benjamin was taken by lot. Then he brought forward the tribe of Benjamin, clan by clan, and Matri's clan was taken. Finally Saul son of Kish was taken. But when they looked for him, he was not to be found.

So they inquired further of the Lord, "Has the man come here yet?"
And the Lord said, "Yes, he has hidden himself among the baggage."

They ran and brought him out, and as he stood among the people he was a head taller than any of the others.

Samuel said to all the people, "Do you see the man the Lord has chosen? There is no one like him among all the people."
Then the people shouted, "Long live the king!" (20-24)

Why on earth was a man just touched with the power of God and changed into a different person hiding in the baggage!?

Saul understandably had a hard time accepting he'd be king, but first he doesn't tell his uncle what happened, and now he's hiding in the baggage, insecure and fearful. Today we might say he had low self-esteem. We'd be sympathetic and recommend therapy, or try to build up his weak ego. But what *self*-image and *self*-esteem are really about is *self*. The focus is off God. Our weaknesses and problems don't just disappear when the Spirit of God comes - but do you act on feelings, or on faith in what God has said? Saul was driven by feelings of incompetency, weakness, and fear. Who's the real Saul? The powerfully anointed king whom they laud? Or the little kid scared to be around people?

If you have a hard time being with people you're going to have a hard time serving God - unless you're called to a monastery! Saul had worked on his father's farm and wasn't used to being around anyone. He'd never been in leadership and had no training to be king. We can hardly blame him for his struggles. Had he really heard God? Was he really chosen to be king? Why would God choose someone so obviously unqualified?

Why? Because God wanted him to see the absolute necessity of living in the Spirit. He couldn't make it as king if he was walking in the flesh. He'd be hiding in the baggage all the time! The only way to handle the immense task before him was to rely on God moment by moment. The same is true for you. God will save you and call you to an impossible task. There's no way you can even be a Christian unless you're walking in the Spirit. You work long and hard to please God - only to fail miserably and wonder if this Christian thing really is for you. It seems like you just can't hack it - and that's exactly where God wants you. The Old Testament graphically shows how we can never measure up to his standards. It's only when we give up our own efforts that we begin to comprehend what being a Christian is all about: Jesus living his life through us.

No offense intended, pastor, but people with no natural talent who look totally unqualified are often called to the ministry. God may pass up born leaders and pick a nobody to head up an important work, because it's so evident they can only make it by totally relying on the Spirit. The highly gifted man struggles with pride and giving up his own efforts, often getting in the way of God's work.

Hopefully you don't have to learn the hard lessons in front of a whole church, or the whole nation. The consequences of walking in the flesh as a shepherd are different from walking in the flesh as king. You might lose a few sheep to a lion as a shepherd, but as king your entire nation can go down in defeat. A nationally televised preacher walking in the flesh will cause a lot more trouble than the pastor of a small church. You affect more people and the damage to God's honor is much greater. The further you go in God the more you have to totally rely on the Spirit. If you're going to make it, there has to be a radical death to self. Saul was too caught up in himself to see God or let him take over. Do you go with your feelings, or believe God? Your experience following a deep encounter with God can go either way. Are you going to start acting like a mighty adopted son of God, designed to reign with Christ? Will you step out in faith in the power of the Spirit? Or, bound by your sin, fear, and feelings of inferiority, stay weak and ineffective, trying to hide, and acting like nothing's changed? Get out of the baggage!

When Saul finally appeared, he was a head taller than anyone else. Samuel proudly said *"there is no one like him among all the people."* Everyone could see how physically capable he was, but, like some of us, he didn't seem to realize it. He acted like a little kid instead of a towering, powerful, man of God. You may have gifts and abilities that are obvious to everyone, but you don't see them because you can't get your eyes off yourself and onto God. Even if Saul was the shortest one there, even if he had no natural ability, the only thing that really mattered was that God had chosen him. And God often chooses the weak to confound the wise.

Grown men in positions of great responsibility still feel that tension. At times we'd love to hide in the baggage or go back to the peaceful pastures. Herd sheep for a while or be a kid again. Great preachers are terrified of getting up in front of a crowd. You may wake up and wonder what on earth you're doing pastoring a church, responsible to God for hundreds of people, or look at your wife and think "who is this woman?" There will be nights when you lie awake with your stomach in knots, feeling very small and weak, thinking about all the problems facing you. At that point you don't need motivational courses or pep talks on how great you are. You probably don't need to go back to school for more training. You need to look to the Lord. Recall his promises, drink deeply of the Spirit's fullness, commune with God, draw strength from the Word, and step out in faith as the powerful man that you are in Jesus Christ.

Scoundrels and Valiant Men

Ready or not, Saul had been presented as Israel's first king.

Samuel explained to the people the rights and duties of kingship. He wrote them down on a scroll and deposited it before the Lord. Then Samuel dismissed the people to go to their own homes.

Saul also went to his home in Gibeah, accompanied by valiant men whose hearts God had touched. But some scoundrels said, "How can this fellow save us?" They despised him and brought him no gifts. But Saul kept silent. (25-27)

There were two very different reactions to Saul.

The first group offered their support. What a difference between these "valiant" men - mature, strong, godly - and immature, cowardly, Saul. Yet, knowing God and understanding and respecting authority, they supported him. It may not have been a natural attraction. They weren't blind. They saw his shyness and inexperience, but they looked beyond that, to what he could become.

When God puts his hand on your life, other men will be drawn to you. Even with Saul's powerful Holy Spirit anointing, God didn't call him and then leave him to fend for himself. Saul's task was to listen to these men, spend time with them, and learn from them. He needed to determine what each had to offer and encourage them to excel at it. One of the marks of a great leader – whether in government, business, or the church – is the quality of men he has around him. A truly gifted leader will draw other gifted men, while an insecure leader will be threatened by them. The real test is not just drawing them, but using them and cultivating their support. God was giving Saul a precious resource – and from all appearances he squandered it. They went home with him, but it's not clear what happened then. Perhaps if Saul had stayed close to them he could have been shielded from the cruel opposition and ridicule of the second group.

Men tend to be independent and resist anyone's help, but God rarely calls a man to solitary leadership. You're part of a body with different ministry gifts. If he calls you to a task, he'll gather other men to help accomplish it. That can be a blow to your pride, since they may be more experienced and qualified than you, but if God's drawing them, that doesn't matter. They may not be the men you'd choose, but God knows what he's doing, and is graciously providing the support and direction you need. Treasure and listen to them, allow them to help you, and humbly thank God for them. Do you have any "valiant men" around you - or any you could seek out? Is it time to start praying for God to send some? Could you be one of the valiant men God would use to encourage someone else?

Not everyone can be king. It may be humbling, but accept whatever calling God has for you. Don't be like the second group, who *"despised him,"* and *"brought him no gifts."* Strong words, to show how strong the opposition was. No matter where you are, you'll have detractors as well as supporters. Saul was no exception. Can you picture a bunch of tough, macho, men in the crowd laughing at this kid who's been dragged out from the baggage? They're troublemakers, and you can expect them when God starts moving in your life. Their purpose is to tear you down, discourage you, and make you question what God has said. They're sent from the accuser of the brethren, who hates God and hates you. We'd love for him to go away, but wherever God is moving, Satan will be there trying to disrupt his work. It would be great if they could hold off until Saul got established, but Satan is no gentleman. If he can derail a work of God at the very outset, he will.

What's sad is these troublemakers were from Saul's own people. It would be understandable if the Philistines refused to bring him gifts - but fellow Israelites? Unfortunately, some of the strongest opposition comes from the church. People walking in pride and the flesh will despise the man God touches and raises up. Few things have more potential for conflict than choosing church leadership. Those who feel passed over or better qualified will often despise the one selected and try to undermine him. They're notably absent at an installation or recognition service where others are bringing gifts.

Why would God allow these troublemakers to come against Saul so quickly? Was he being cruel and uncaring? Definitely not. An important part of growth and leadership is dealing with opposition. Much as you'd like to, you can't avoid the battle! God faithfully provided valiant men. Now the question is who Saul will listen to. How will he respond to the troublemakers? How much will he allow God to minister to him through the valiant men?

Saul kept silent

Once again, Saul kept silent. Men are good at that.[20] It seems the easy way out. At times we talk too much, but sometimes we're silent when we need to speak. Was Saul showing wise restraint, as Jesus did with his accusers? Or was he just scared and didn't know what to say? He probably should have said something, maybe returning blessing for the curses. My guess is he felt inadequate. Instead of confronting them, or talking to God, who would have reassured him, Saul internalized it, wearing down an already weak ego a little more. Their voices joined those of his father, friends, and anyone else who may have put him down as a kid. As he returned home their words kept ringing in his ears, while the words of the valiant men didn't seem as strong. The experience with Samuel seemed distant, but his accusers seemed very present. Satan began building a stronghold in his mind on the foundation of his own personality issues. Later on, as his rule crumbled, their words may have kept coming back to him. God provided a way out, but as we see Saul's life unfold, the battle only intensified.

Have you struggled with the same voices? You may have let go of valiant men God brought into your life - too proud, independent, and scared of relationships with other men to reach out to them. Meanwhile the voice of the troublemakers has remained strong, joining those taunting voices from earlier in your life, saying you'll never make it or amount to anything. You may feel there's something different about you. You'll never have victory. There's no hope for you.

You're not different. Every man from Adam on down has experienced it. You have the choice of listening to what God has said, or to the accuser and his troublemakers who despise you. Identify the voice of your accuser. Tell him you know where that voice is coming from, and decide to reject his taunts from now on. Instead of meditating on peoples' ridicule and your bad experiences, meditate on what God has said about you in his Word. Pray that God would graciously provide valiant men around you, because you can't make it on your own.

Have you been hiding in the baggage while God is calling you to step out and powerfully impact your family and your world? What are you afraid of? The taunts of the enemy? God is with you! He'll supply all the support you need as you step out in faith.

Chapter 5

Saul's Big Comeback:
1 Samuel 11:1-11

So far things haven't looked too good for King Saul. His dramatic experience with God didn't seem to last. Had God made a mistake choosing him? Was there any hope for him? Israel's enemies were laughing at the new king - a cowardly kid. It's the perfect time to attack.

Nahash the Ammonite went up and besieged Jabesh Gilead. And all the men of Jabesh said to him, "Make a treaty with us, and we will be subject to you."

But Nahash the Ammonite replied, "I will make a treaty with you only on the condition that I gouge out the right eye of every one of you and so bring disgrace on all Israel."

The elders of Jabesh said to him, "Give us seven days so we can send messengers throughout Israel; if no one comes to rescue us, we will surrender to you." (1-3)

As usual, Saul was nowhere to be seen. With no leadership and no hope of victory, Jabesh didn't even want to fight. Submitting to Nahash, the Ammonite king, meant virtual slavery, but even that wasn't enough for him. He wants to disgrace Israel by gouging out every man's right eye. He probably would have ended up killing them all.

It's not that different today. Strong, godly, leaders are few, leaving us vulnerable to the enemy's attacks. Instead of fighting Satan, we surrender to him or make little deals with him, allowing certain sins to remain. We give him parts of our lives because we're tired of fighting. That's risky. When you make one concession he wants more. A finger hold becomes a stronghold. Your deal with Satan can bring disgrace on Jesus Christ and his church, as we've seen only too often. He won't be satisfied until you're dead.

Jabesh wasn't quite ready to concede defeat, though. In desperation they sent messengers throughout Israel, in the unlikely chance someone would come to help. Apparently they didn't even think about Saul or expect help from their king.

When the messengers came to Gibeah of Saul and reported these terms to the people, they all wept aloud. Just then Saul was returning from the fields, behind his oxen, and he asked, "What is wrong with everyone? Why are they weeping?" Then they repeated to him what the men of Jabesh had said. (4-5)

What was Saul doing in the fields? It sounds like he forgot about being chosen king. It was back to business as usual. It happens to many Christians - a spiritual awakening followed by a flurry of activity. People talk about how you've become a Christian and may make fun of you. Like Saul, you get anointed and baptized - everything you're supposed to do - but then slip back into your old life as if nothing ever happened.

Saul was changed into a new person and told to do whatever his hands found to do, because God was with him. But was plowing the field the best thing he could find to do? Maybe Israel wouldn't have been humiliated before her enemy if Saul had been on the job.

When Saul heard their words, the Spirit of God came powerfully upon him, and he burned with anger. He took a pair of oxen, cut them into pieces, and sent the pieces by messengers throughout Israel, proclaiming, "This is what will be done to the oxen of anyone who does not follow Saul and Samuel." (6-7)

Saul may have forgotten his call, but God hadn't forgotten him. Saul wasn't in church or seeking God. There were no prophets around. He didn't do anything. He was just bringing in the oxen when he heard the people weeping, and that stirred something deep in his spirit. Let God stir your spirit as you hear about the needs of his people! Don't become hardened to the suffering around you!

What could make a kid out in the field with his oxen, seemingly a total failure as king, suddenly change into a mighty warrior? The Holy Spirit had filled him when he left Samuel. Now the Spirit *came powerfully upon him* - again. He was changed into a different person.

Saul had been silent before his accusers, but suddenly he got in touch with his anger. Has anger caused you so much trouble you try to avoid it? If you're stifling it, you may be stifling godly passion. The Lord can use righteous anger - at the enemy, injustice, and sin - to spur us to action. Saul cut up the oxen he'd just brought in from the field. They'd been an important part of his life, but he won't need them anymore. Would anyone follow this young king who had never done anything? No problem there.

Then the terror of the Lord fell on the people, and they came out together as one. When Saul mustered them at Bezek, the men of Israel numbered three hundred thousand and those of Judah thirty thousand.

They told the messengers who had come, "Say to the men of Jabesh Gilead, 'By the time the sun is hot tomorrow, you will be rescued.'" When the messengers went and reported this to the men of Jabesh, they were elated. They said to the Ammonites, "Tomorrow we will surrender to you, and you can do to us whatever you like."

The next day Saul separated his men into three divisions; during the last watch of the night they broke into the camp of the Ammonites and slaughtered them until the heat of the day. Those who survived were scattered, so that no two of them were left together. (7-11)

We could use some terror of God today. We seem to have lost the fear of the Lord.[21] Saul got his army - 330,000 strong - almost overnight! But now there's another problem. As far as we know, he'd never fought anything more than wild animals, let alone lead a vast army against experienced warriors. Once again, that's no problem. The Spirit of God not only stirred him to anger, he was equipped for battle and made a confident leader. In bold faith, word was sent to Jabesh they'd be delivered by noon the next day. Sure enough, Saul led the army in a decisive victory, and the city was freed. What an incredible turnaround!

You can experience the same power

Are you facing a new challenge that feels like more than you can handle? This was at least the second time the Spirit had come upon Saul. Up to this point he'd effectively quenched the Spirit, or maybe there had never been a chance for his power to be demonstrated. You may remember being filled with the Spirit years ago, but now that experience seems dry and distant. You need the Spirit to come upon you with power - for the first time, or the fiftieth. A daily walk in the power of the Holy Spirit is your best defense against the enemy's attacks. If you want to experience his power, get out on the front lines and fight the enemy. Find out what God is doing and identify with his people. If you're not in a place where God can use you in witness or ministry you may never experience the Spirit's fullness. It's not about getting certain gifts or feeling good; the Spirit empowers you for a task as you step out in faith.

Saul's plans for the night - and for months to come - were dramatically interrupted, like the fishermen who dropped everything to follow Jesus. Are you willing to have your plans dramatically changed?

We're not called to judge or condemn a part of the body that comes under attack. Other Jews didn't point fingers or call Jabesh weak because the enemy came against them, yet that's what we do with other Christians. Intercede for them and do what you can to help them, instead of condemning them!

Have you felt a holy anger about what's happening in the church or in our nation? When the Spirit comes you should find yourself stirred at the enemy's challenges. Could God use you to call his people to action? Why not? Saul demanded everyone to be part of the effort or have his oxen cut up! The people turned out as one man. There's no indication Saul had to go out and chop up any oxen! A Spirit-anointed man will draw people together to fight. Unity is built around a task, and that unity is more urgent in battle.

What kind of impact would we have on this country if believers joined together as one man? Can you imagine the victory over the enemy? May the fear - terror! - of God fall on the church so we'd put aside our differences, fight the enemy together, and see God's deliverance.

What an amazing comeback from hiding in the baggage! Like Saul, we've all blown it. It's part of being human. It can start you on a downward spiral, feeling like you've gone too far and there's no return. You can accept the lies that you have to work your way back, or that God will never use you again. But God's there waiting, longing for you to return and take your rightful place in the family. He's reaching into your cold, hurting, heart. As quickly as you fell, you can be back with the Lord, ready for battle.

Chapter 6

The Importance of Mercy: 1 Samuel 11: 12-15

Saul's approval rating soared, along with his confidence and self-image. Suddenly he's a hero, and the people are ready to take drastic action against those who questioned choosing him as king. *The people then said to Samuel, "Who was it that asked, 'Shall Saul reign over us?' Turn these men over to us so that we may put them to death."* (12)

It's odd they came to Samuel with their request, although Saul was young, and maybe they still regarded the aged prophet as their leader. But Samuel didn't have a chance to respond. Something had changed. *But Saul said, "No one will be put to death today, for this day the Lord has rescued Israel."* (13)

We can only guess at the anger and shame Saul internalized as he kept silent when the troublemakers ridiculed him. Now the people want to kill them. The cowardly Saul would have jumped at the opportunity to let someone do his dirty work, but this is a different Saul, who refuses to have Jewish blood mar his great God-given victory. He chooses to show mercy.

You may carry vivid memories of the parent who abused you. The teacher who made fun of you in front of the whole class. The co-worker who destroyed your reputation to get your promotion. The man who ran off with your wife. There's tremendous power in that hurt and anger, and revenge can feel very attractive. How you handle offense and injustice will have a big impact on your growth in Christ and the proper use of your kingly authority.

Three ways to respond to hurt

Saul's first approach, in I Samuel 10, was to internalize the anger. He stood there silent, paralyzed and powerless, like a little kid who can't talk back to his dad or the neighborhood bully. Jesus did teach us to turn the other cheek[22] - but we do that from a position of strength. Saul's namesake, the Apostle Paul, was well acquainted with being tormented by troublemakers. He'd also been one, standing in approval as Stephen was stoned. Later he wrote: *If it is possible, as far as it depends on you, live at peace with everyone. Do not take revenge, my dear friends, but leave room for God's wrath, for it is written: "It is mine to avenge; I will repay," says the Lord. On the contrary: "If your enemy is hungry, feed him; if he is thirsty, give him something to drink. In doing this, you will heap burning coals on his head."*[23]

Don't confuse internalizing your anger, as Saul did, with turning the other cheek and allowing God to avenge.

Later in his life Saul took almost the opposite approach. When the Holy Spirit left him he became consumed with jealousy and trying to kill David, his perceived enemy. If you're not walking in the Spirit, you may devote great energy, time, and even money trying to get even with those who've wronged you. It's human nature to want justice, but your judgment is clouded by your hurt and damaged ego. How would you respond if someone offered to punish those who have wronged you? The Israelites expected Saul to thank them: "Wow, you're a really loyal subject. Let me give you an important place in my new administration." It might have been a way of seeking his favor.

But in one of the only glimpses of real character in Saul, he took a third way. Looking past the offense, he chose mercy, and stopped the talk of revenge. When God's given you victory, there's no need to go back and open up old wounds. Some would say a real man expresses his anger and avenges himself on his enemies. But, with God's help, Saul took the stronger – and harder – route, forgiving those who had wronged him and showing them mercy.

God can give you the power to forgive, love your enemies, and pray for those who persecute you. He saved you by his mercy and grace when you were in bondage, choosing to overlook how deeply you'd wronged him. When you realize you're as sinful as those who've hurt you, it's hard to condemn them. You can let go of your anger and desire for revenge. When God has changed your life and given you victory there's no need to hunt down old enemies and settle old debts. Let them go, and let God deal with them.

Are you afraid they'll hurt you again or take advantage of you? We don't know how these men responded, but there's no record of further trouble from them. With Saul's victory and newfound character, the scoffers may have been convicted of their attitudes - or even become his supporters. As Saul acted with integrity, their continued attacks would only make them look weak.

A call to celebrate

Saul had a slow start, dominated by his immaturity, shyness, and the taunts of the troublemakers. But now he's changed, and Samuel, in his wisdom, realized it was time to celebrate.

Then Samuel said to the people, "Come, let us go to Gilgal and there renew the kingship."

So all the people went to Gilgal and made Saul king in the presence of the Lord. There they sacrificed fellowship offerings before the Lord, and Saul and all the Israelites held a great celebration. (14-15)

Samuel didn't want a king, but now he leads the way in reaffirming the kingship. Gilgal was an appropriate place, since it was there Joshua set up the twelve stones after Israel crossed the Jordan into the promised land, *"so that all the peoples of the earth might know that the hand of the Lord is powerful, and so that you might always fear the Lord your God."* [24]

There would probably have been no celebration had Saul killed the troublemakers. When you're bent on revenge it's hard to come into the Lord's presence, but as you worship God you'll forget about those who wronged you. Showing mercy as Saul did produces joy. With worship and feasting they rejoiced in God's goodness, faithfulness, and provision. Being in his presence doesn't have to be solemn. Jews love to celebrate. We could use more celebrations in our churches!

Samuel had another reason for calling the people to Gilgal. Now that Saul had shown he could be an effective king, Samuel felt it was time to step down, although he would continue mentoring Saul. He used this gathering to deliver his farewell speech.

Is there someone you need to show mercy?

You may try to forget about it, push it deep inside, or rehearse it over and over. You may be tempted to take things into your own hands and get even with the person who wronged you, either through character assassination or actually harming them. You may be consumed by the need for vengeance, as Saul was later. But those things don't work. It's not that your anger isn't justified. No one would say what they did to you was right, but God is calling you to take a very bold and strong stand. Decide you won't seek revenge. Ask for God's help. As he's forgiven you, choose to show mercy, and forgive. You'll feel such a tremendous release you too will want to worship and celebrate in the Lord's presence.

Chapter 7

Samuel's Farewell Speech:
1 Samuel 12:1-25

What do you long to hear from your spiritual father? Or from your dad? Israel's just had a family celebration. They're feeling good. They have a king! They defeated the Ammonites! Things are really looking up for them. They eagerly gather to get their father's blessing.

Samuel said to all Israel, "I have listened to everything you said to me and have set a king over you. Now you have a king as your leader. As for me, I am old and gray, and my sons are here with you. I have been your leader from my youth until this day. Here I stand. Testify against me in the presence of the Lord and his anointed. Whose ox have I taken? Whose donkey have I taken? Whom have I cheated? Whom have I oppressed? From whose hand have I accepted a bribe to make me shut my eyes? If I have done any of these things, I will make it right." (1-3)

Not quite what they were expecting to hear, but old men have a tendency to get grumpy. You know what happens to a man through the years? He tries hard to be everything a man should be. A good husband and father. Successful at work and financially comfortable. If he's a believer, a good Christian and leader in the church. But over the years this intense jumble of emotions grows which he finds difficult to express or even understand. There are the failures and rejections. Deep love for his wife - but longing for greater intimacy. Worry over the direction his kids are taking. Time passing too quickly, and feeling out of control. You mix all that - and more - together and it can come out grumpy. Many men just withdraw into their "man cave" and shut down. But look beyond the hurt and need for love and affirmation. Chances are he still has something important to say. We may placate old men to shut them up so we don't have to listen to their complaints. Part of us wishes they'd just go away. That's what happened here. You can tell by how quickly they give Samuel what they think he wants to hear.

"You have not cheated or oppressed us," they replied. "You have not taken anything from anyone's hand." (4)

Now Samuel knows they haven't heard his heart. He's not about to shut up, so he pulls out the God card, which is often quite effective in producing guilt. The excitement's gone and they feel small - like a little kid scolded by mommy or daddy. It's tough to be reminded of your sin. You wish you could forget it and everything would be fine again, but it doesn't work that way. You can't move on until you deal with it. Deep inside you know you did wrong. Your wife, your boss - God - has every reason to get down on you. In frustration you may ask "What more do you want from me?" But there's no way around coming clean and dealing with the consequences.

Samuel said to them, "The Lord is witness against you, and also his anointed is witness this day, that you have not found anything in my hand."
"He is witness," they said.

Then Samuel said to the people, "It is the Lord who appointed Moses and Aaron and brought your ancestors up out of Egypt. Now then, stand here, because I am going to confront you with evidence before the Lord as to all the righteous acts performed by the Lord for you and your ancestors." (5-7)

Behind all the judgmental talk and grumpiness, Samuel's concerned about where they're at with the Lord. He feels partly responsible for it. For years he's faithfully preached God's word and they still haven't gotten it. Now he's stepping out of the picture. His sons can't take his place. It's not until David's reign that another prominent prophet arises. He knows Saul's stepping into a tough situation. It will be a huge help to the new king if the people are right with God, and he knows they need revival. If he can leave them with that he'll rest easier.

"Now then, stand still and see this great thing the Lord is about to do before your eyes! Is it not wheat harvest now? I will call on the Lord to send thunder and rain. And you will realize what an evil thing you did in the eyes of the Lord when you asked for a king." Then Samuel called on the Lord, and that same day the Lord sent thunder and rain. So all the people stood in awe of the Lord and of Samuel. The people all said to Samuel, "Pray to the Lord your God for your servants so that we will not die, for we have added to all our other sins the evil of asking for a king." (16-19)

What do you think of Samuel calling down thunder and rain? Too sensational? It definitely took faith! But God honored his request! Samuel wasn't on an ego trip, and now God has their attention.   Sure, Samuel let his personal issues affect his message. But who doesn't? Once that's cleared away, we see his great wisdom - and a path we can still follow today to get right with God. Israel's history would have been far different if Saul and the rest of the nation had followed what Samuel laid out. It's essentially what should happen in church every week, or when we get together with God for a daily quiet time:

- You get a fresh view of whom God is as you worship him, see his power revealed, or read the Bible.

- You have a chance to humble yourself, be honest, and confess your sin. But it doesn't end there - God calls you to repentance, to stop what you're doing wrong, turn around, and follow him.

- God teaches you a new way to live, through your own study of the Word, the preaching and teaching in church, and the leading of his Holy Spirit. Then you must decide what you're going to do.

Be awed by God's power

Samuel had challenged them with their sin. The Israelites thought everything was great, but they were leaving God out of the picture. They'd hoped for a nice blessing from Samuel, a feel-good sermon, so they could be on their way and keep doing what they felt like doing. They need a reminder of whom God is. It's easy to forget he's the all-powerful creator and Lord of the universe, and we're his sinful creation. A potentially damaging storm would display God's power, vindicate Samuel, and convict the people of their offense in asking for a king. It almost never rained in Canaan during the harvest, so the rain and thunder have the intended effect.

Are you like the Israelites, self-confidently going to church, looking for your blessing? Have you been around God so long you've forgotten who he is? It's easy to think everything's fine - when actually you have serious issues with the Lord. He has to wake you up to see a holy, all-powerful God - and the depth of your sin against him. Do you sense any awe or fear of God? When was the last time you witnessed his power and were reminded of his greatness? Has he ever used a dramatic sign to get your attention - or does he need to now?

God's ready to forgive them, but they've never acknowledged how they rejected him when they asked for a king. Moving on starts with true repentance.

Repentance

Realizing their mistake, they humbly ask Samuel to intercede for them. We might expect him to take advantage of the opportunity and come down on them again, but now he gives godly, fatherly advice. It may not be the pep talk they hoped for, but it's the truth, and that's what we need. We might not like everything the Bible says, but God is fair. He's given us his Word to teach us right and wrong, and made clear what he expects of us. The problem is we often don't want to obey.

"If you fear the Lord and serve and obey him and do not rebel against his commands, and if both you and the king who reigns over you follow the Lord your God—good! But if you do not obey the Lord, and if you rebel against his commands, his hand will be against you, as it was against your ancestors." (14-15)

"Do not be afraid. "You have done all this evil; yet do not turn away from the Lord, but serve the Lord with all your heart. Do not turn away after useless idols. They can do you no good, nor can they rescue you, because they are useless. For the sake of his great name the Lord will not reject his people, because the Lord was pleased to make you his own. As for me, far be it from me that I should sin against the Lord by failing to pray for you. And I will teach you the way that is good and right. But be sure to fear the Lord and serve him faithfully with all your heart; consider what great things he has done for you. Yet if you persist in doing evil, both you and your king will perish." (20-25)

Having acknowledged who God is, and that we need his grace, we're ready to move on. He reassures us of his love and care, and gives three pieces of wise counsel to help us make it.

Serve the Lord wholeheartedly

Now they've set things right with God, they can serve him. It's not enough just to believe in him, or even reluctantly serve him - we're to serve him with *all our heart*. By nature, we don't want anyone to tell us what to do. We want to do our own thing. That was the reason we fell in the first place! Deciding to walk in obedience is essential to overcoming our rebellious nature. Now they have a king, and both the king *and* the people must follow

God. That means the whole nation will suffer under an ungodly king, and if they persist in doing evil even a godly king will not save them. Israel's history is full of both experiences.

Stay close to God

The key to making it is staying close to God. There are two dangers to watch for here.

First, turning away from the Lord. Some people get discouraged when confronted with their sin and feel they can never make it as a Christian. But no matter how serious your sin, God will take you back. He loves you and rejoices at your repentance. You're his adopted son, and his reputation is at stake. He doesn't want anyone talking about how badly he treats his people.

The second danger is allowing useless idols to pull you away from God. Samuel was probably thinking of carved images, but our idols are a little different today: Money, women, fame, houses, cars, the internet. It may be good in itself, but becomes an idol and is destructive and useless if it's more important than God. Rather than deal with sin and walk with God, the temptation is to fill your life with work, women, or some project - usually something you can control.

Don't play with God

The consequences of disobedience are serious:

- God's hand will be against you. If you've ever experienced that, it's not fun. Life becomes miserable.

- Everything you try to do is frustrated. If that's not bad enough, you'll be swept away.

- Finally, you'll be destroyed.

That's not just for Saul and the Israelites. That still applies today if you turn away from the Lord. Don't play with God!

Unfortunately, even though there were bright spots here and there, Israel couldn't make these simple choices. God was so serious about helping them he sent his own Son to die for them - and you! It's only in a relationship with Jesus you'll find the power and ability to live this out. Praise God for Jesus! Not only did he send his own Son, he sent the Holy Spirit to live inside you and empower you to do the right thing.

The leader's responsibility

It took a minute for him to get going, but Samuel hit a home run with this sermon, faithfully sharing God's heart one last time. Even though it's his farewell message, it's not the end of his ministry. He'll continue to do two critical things essential for anyone in Christian leadership:

First, pray for the people. A good way to evaluate a leader is to look at his prayer life. Samuel says that failing to pray is sinning against the Lord. If you haven't been praying for your people – or your family - you're depriving them of something very important. Confess it to God as sin.

Second, teach them what is good and right. The leader who doesn't teach his people basic right and wrong has failed. Too many pastors are scared to do what Samuel did here! You may be clumsy with it, as Samuel was, but God will use you. Your church deserves the truth.

Do you need a fresh encounter with God?

If you've been trying to make it on your own as a Christian, it's impossible. There's nothing wrong with you. You just can't do it by yourself. Maybe you've never asked Jesus into your life or experienced the power of the Holy Spirit enabling you to follow him. You thought you could make it on your own, but God's convicted you of your need for him. Ask him to forgive you and fill you with his Spirit.

Do you need a fresh vision of God? Have you grown distant from him? Do you know where you're at with Christ? Does the idea of living in the supernatural seem foreign to you? Maybe you thought you were doing great - while in reality there are things in your life God's upset about. Maybe you suspect he's mad at you. Ask his Holy Spirit to search your heart, and genuinely repent if that's necessary. It's time to get serious about obedience, seek God with all your heart, and put aside any useless idols you've turned to. God's not going to reject you, but before you can move on you need to honestly acknowledge and confess any sin.

PART TWO

A dam lost Eden and was condemned to hard labor for the rest of his life. Yet he never lost his mandate to reign. In fact, God still had plans to extend man's dominion way beyond birds and fish:

"You [Christ] have made them to be a kingdom and priests to serve our God, and they will reign on the earth." (Revelation 5:10)

You are now a prince and priest in service to almighty God. As you exercise kingly authority, he's preparing you to reign on earth:

They will be priests of God and of Christ and will reign with him for a thousand years. (Revelation 20:6)

That authority will expand even further. What started with caring for his creation becomes sharing in Christ's reign for all eternity:

And they will reign for ever and ever. (Revelation 22:5)

That's awesome. Are you ready for it? It calls for intensive training, and God is using the situations in your life right now to prepare you. The challenge can be keeping your eyes on that throne when this world offers so much to distract you.

Typically starting in your thirties and increasingly stretching into the fifties, in many ways this second part of your journey is the best time of your life. It's summer, or, if you think of life as a day, it's 9-5. Hopefully you're walking with God, settled in your calling and career. Traditionally your family is a big part of your life and happiness.

Unfortunately, as great as life should be at this point, it's often a time of testing. If you're like many men, you may struggle with attraction to other women as your wife's imperfections become more apparent. Divorce may even be mentioned. Your teenagers test your patience and break your heart. You might put on more weight than you'd like, overindulging in unhealthy food. Although you're surrounded by people, you may be too busy to feel close to any of them. Time's moving on. You thought you'd have it more together by now. Change comes harder, and you're more aware of your limitations. You can't afford to waste opportunities or make big mistakes. Your legacy is unclear, although you get glimpses of how the story ends. You're facing who you really are - and it's not all good. You either choose to make adjustments and get healthier - or settle into unhealthy patterns that will be hard to break.

As he begins this second journey, Saul seems poised to come into his own as king. He has God's promises and anointing and Samuel's support. The people love him. He's raised an effective army and won an important battle. But instead of establishing his kingdom and using his authority for the good of the nation, things start falling apart. In place of strength we see cowardice. Saul's unresolved issues become painfully apparent as he makes one bad decision after another. His story is full of lessons on what can go wrong in the prime of your life.

Chapter 8

Saul Loses the Kingdom:
1 Samuel 13:1-15

Saul was thirty years old when he became king, and he reigned over Israel forty- two years. (1)

Saul's already been king for a while, so why would the Bible give this kind of summary statement, which usually comes at the beginning or end of a king's reign? The inspired author is letting us know this is a turning point. It's the start of Saul's second journey. He had a long reign, but it was more like a long prison sentence, marked by poor decisions. The game goes on for many years, but he already knows he can't win. Right here, early on, he makes the mistake that costs him the kingdom. Listen up. This may be an important decision time for you. Will you make the same mistake? Many men do. Or will you keep growing in your kingly authority? Maybe you've lost what was once a powerful ministry. This may help you see what went wrong, and how God can restore what you lost. He delights in giving second chances. He even gave Saul another chance. Just don't do what Saul did and blow that one too. Learn from your mistakes.

The scene's familiar: the Philistines are preparing for war. Saul can rid Israel of them once and for all. He's just seen God's power devastate the Ammonites. But before the battle even begins he made a critical error. *Saul chose three thousand men from Israel; two thousand were with him at Mikmash and in the hill country of Bethel, and a thousand were with Jonathan at Gibeah in Benjamin. The rest of the men he sent back to their homes.* (2)

God's Spirit played such a key role in the last victory, but now he's totally out of the picture. No mention of prayer or any divine guidance. Saul is confident - cocky - after his great victory at Jabesh, and makes a foolish decision to send the troops home. Then he gives a third of the remaining men to his young son. Jonathan had great potential, but Saul never bothered providing the leadership and covering he needed, so in youthful zeal he acted on his own. Providing direction and support to the people under you is a key part of wisely using your authority.

Jonathan attacked the Philistine outpost at Geba, and the Philistines heard about it. Then Saul had the trumpet blown throughout the land and said, "Let the Hebrews hear!" So all Israel heard the news: "Saul has attacked the Philistine outpost, and now Israel has become obnoxious to the Philistines." And the people were summoned to join Saul at Gilgal. (3-4)

The news release mistakenly said Saul led the attack. Even though it was ill advised, he wants to get the glory for any victory. Jonathan may have had good intentions, but there's no indication God was leading him. With things looking ugly, Saul soon found himself in the awkward position of calling back the troops he'd just sent home. Hastily reversing decisions you've just made is not usually a sign of good leadership.

The Philistines assembled to fight Israel, with three thousand chariots, six thousand charioteers, and soldiers as numerous as the sand on the seashore. They went up and camped at Mikmash, east of Beth Aven. When the Israelites saw that their situation was critical and that their army was hard pressed, they hid in caves and thickets, among the rocks, and in pits and cisterns. Some Hebrews even crossed the Jordan to the land of Gad and Gilead. Saul remained at Gilgal, and all the troops with him were quaking with fear. (5-7)

Saul had only three thousand men at this point, outnumbered two to one with charioteers alone! Philistine soldiers were as numerous as the sand on the seashore - a biblical way of saying they were too many to count. No wonder the Israelites were afraid! But hiding in pits, cisterns, and caves? Or leaving the area completely? That's pathetic and cowardly! What a contrast to Saul's boldness at Jabesh! Where was the Spirit's power now? What happened to the leadership that inspired courage and drew men around him? We're back to the cowardly Saul hiding in the baggage!

What made the difference?

Something was wrong, or his men wouldn't be quaking with paralyzing fear. That's definitely not from the Spirit of God. In fact, this time the Holy Spirit isn't even mentioned. What happened to the Spirit's anointing? How could things change so dramatically, so quickly? Saul still had God-given kingly authority. God was just as able to defeat his enemies. Sure, this vast army was intimidating, but Saul had seen God gather and equip a powerful army. The only change was in Saul.

Saul felt good after his great victory, let his guard down, and sent most of his troops home. He didn't want to think about fighting for a while. While Saul figured out how to respond to the attack, Jonathan boldly moved against an enemy outpost. Satan may not mind when you sit back and take it easy, but it's another story to step into his territory. When he's been defeated in battle he doesn't just back off and leave you alone. He comes back even stronger, trying to catch you off balance with circumstances that look overwhelming, to discourage you and fill you with fear. Or he may try a subtle approach. He targets the leader. If he can disable the king, the whole nation will suffer. Since Saul had left God out of the picture, Satan can sow fear in the troops and exploit his weaknesses, which are more evident under pressure.

Saul's fatal mistake

Saul may have sent for Samuel when things started getting rough. Samuel commanded him to wait seven days to make a sacrifice - further discouraging the troops and setting the stage for a small mistake that would cost Saul his kingdom, and eventually his life.

He waited seven days, the time set by Samuel; but Samuel did not come to Gilgal, and Saul's men began to scatter. So he said, "Bring me the burnt offering and the fellowship offerings." And Saul offered up the burnt offering. (8-9)

Do you know what a double-bind is? You're between a rock and a hard place. No matter what you do, it's wrong. Either way you lose. Saul felt that double-bind. On one hand, the Philistines were waiting to attack him. On the other hand, his troops were full of fear - starting to desert him and scatter because of the delay. Saul knew he needed God, and Samuel represented God's strength and stability. He was counting on him to save the day and gain God's favor - but Samuel let him down and didn't show up on time! Who knows what happened to him? Saul decides his only option is to make the offerings himself. It doesn't sound that serious. After all, he wasn't running after another god or going into battle in his own strength. He was making offerings and seeking God.

Samuel shows up

Wouldn't you know it, *just as he finished making the offering, Samuel arrived, and Saul went out to greet him.* (10) It was probably only an hour or so. Talk about perfect timing! Perfectly bad, that is. Do you think God may have allowed the delay to test Saul? Could he be testing your willingness to wait right now?

As Samuel appeared, relief swept over Saul. Everything would be okay now. Samuel was finally there! Saul ran out to meet him, unaware of having done anything wrong. Or did he know - and was just trying to look good? Samuel knew immediately. He may have seen the smoke going up from the offering.

"What have you done?" asked Samuel. Saul replied, "When I saw that the men were scattering, and that you did not come at the set time, and that the Philistines were assembling at Mikmash, I thought, 'Now the Philistines will come down against me at Gilgal, and I have not sought the lord's favor.' So I felt compelled to offer the burnt offering." (11-12)

Saul's a lot like us - he tries to cover himself and look good. Always ready with an excuse, this one sounded good: "You wouldn't believe how bad things were. The Philistines were ready to fight. And these Israelites! They were leaving me! Of course I had to seek the Lord's favor before going into battle, so I offered the sacrifice."

Sounded good, but something was terribly wrong. He'd already been assured of the Lord's favor.[25] And why did he have to wait this long to pray? Why did he have to offer sacrifices? What was keeping him from gathering his scared troops and seeking God? And why would he say he was "compelled?" Who compelled him? It certainly wasn't the Lord.

"You have done a foolish thing," Samuel said. "You have not kept the command the lord your God gave you; if you had, he would have established your kingdom over Israel for all time. But now your kingdom will not endure; the lord has sought out a man after his own heart and appointed him ruler of his people, because you have not kept the lord's command." (13-14)

Saul disobeyed God. He took it upon himself to think things through and make his own decision. The consequences of that one small act were drastic. Saul could have had an everlasting kingdom. The messiah could have come from his family line. But God needed a man after his own heart in leadership, especially as the nation's first king. Saul wasn't it, and as a result the kingdom would be taken from him.

Then Samuel left Gilgal and went up to Gibeah in Benjamin, and Saul counted the men who were with him. They numbered about six hundred. (15)

Having dropped that bomb, Samuel took off and left Saul with a dis-spirited army to fight a major battle. It's hard to fight when you've just gotten that news and you don't have God's Spirit. The first thing Saul did was count his troops. More than two thirds of his men had deserted. It's that kind of incredibly depressing, discouraging, scene that can make you contemplate suicide.

Do you feel a little sorry for Saul? I've had Christians let me down and can sympathize with his frustration. He was in a really tight spot, and it seems nowhere near as bad as David's adultery and murder. Saul wasn't even given the chance to repent, as David was. It can seem like God had it in for poor Saul, but if you think back on what we've learned about him, this wasn't an isolated experience. When he got home from learning he'd be king, he chose not to tell his uncle what God had done. He hid in the baggage when it was time to anoint him. He didn't know how to deal with opposition. This was just one in a series of unfortunate events.

How to avoid Saul's mistakes and maintain a powerful walk in the Spirit

1. Obedience

You may be tested like Saul - and have Samuel show up at the wrong time. Can you imagine Jesus coming back - just as you've decided to do your own thing? American Christians are experts at designer religion, but Saul's story shows how dangerous that is. Saul was seeking God's favor. It doesn't seem like such a major sin, but obedience is major to God. You may protest that we're saved by faith and not by works, and God understands our weaknesses. True, but that doesn't change how serious he is about obedience. It's not an option. We have to do things his way.

Be careful of your knowledge outstripping your obedience. Have you ever left a conference with notebooks full of exciting things about the Christian life - but not put any of it into practice? That's dangerous! The late British pastor John Stott wrote that the greatest thing hindering the fullness of the Spirit in our lives is too much knowledge.[26] We simply don't walk in all the knowledge we have, which may be why young Christians who don't know that much often experience more of the Spirit. They eagerly put what they learn into practice.

2. Knowing God's Will

If God is that serious about obedience, make it your business to find out what he wants you to do. Diligently study the Word, seek his direction in prayer, and then do what he shows you. Don't ever feel that you're somehow entitled to God's anointing. Look how quickly Saul lost it. You may not lose your salvation, but the Bible never says you can't lose the Spirit's fullness.

3. Staying on the Front Lines

If you want that anointing, stay on the front lines. God gives us his Spirit so we'll do something with his power. Saul was backing off from the battle just as Jonathan was moving into the thick of it. The more you're on the front lines in spiritual battles, witnessing to people and praying for them, the more you'll experience the Spirit. Sure, you can feel the Spirit in church or in your prayer time, but it doesn't compare with preaching the Gospel in enemy territory, or freeing people from their bondages.

Living with the consequences of disobedience

How could Saul reign forty-two years if God was taking the kingdom from him? It was decades before that judgment was carried out. We see his desperation at many points, but forty years is a long time to put on a show of being on top of things as king. He kept plodding through his duties - without the Spirit's anointing. Many Christian leaders and pastors are like Saul. Perhaps you are. They've lost God's anointing through their disobedience but aren't broken over their sin. They try to prop up the appearance of a powerful ministry for years - completely in the flesh. Things may look good to the undiscerning eye, but there's no life, and no move of God.

God is serious about obedience. Where are you at?

- Do you feel you have everything you need from God?

- Are you a little cocky, like Saul after that first victory? Or are you broken and humble before God?

- Have you disobeyed God and lost the fullness of his Spirit?

- Is your response to humbly acknowledge the sin, or try to cover it over and excuse it?

- Are you facing battles with the enemy - defeated and scared like Saul and his men?

- Are you propping up a ministry in your own strength – maybe even unaware the anointing's gone?

Don't waste any time. God's calling you. It's not too late to repent of doing your own thing and get serious about obedience. He'll restore you, fill you with his Spirit, and send you out into battle once again.

Chapter 9

How to Win Battles:
1 Samuel 13:16-22

R eader's Digest used to have a feature called "Drama in Real Life" about people who somehow survived nearly impossible situations. (No one lived to tell about the ones who didn't!) I remember reading about a boat that sank off the coast of Maine. It was so cold, water was freezing all over it. The ocean was covered with sea smoke —a dense fog. Three men ended up in the water, but a flashlight miraculously froze to one of their caps and stayed on. In that thick sea smoke, two other boats found them.

There's one thing that always bothered me about those stories. So many times common sense would have avoided the drama. I even wrote Reader's Digest suggesting they print a sidebar on how to avoid those situations, but they never did. The obvious lesson in the boat story: don't go out on the Atlantic in a small boat at night when the weather forecast is so bad.

Saul fails to prepare for battle

How well we do in our own "drama in real life" depends largely on what we've done *before* the drama.[27] Most of us sail along when the weather's good with little thought about preparing for that freak storm. When it comes, we go crazy and may die because we're not prepared. Saul wasn't, and now he faced almost sure disaster. He'd failed as king and just been told he'd lose his kingdom because of his disobedience. Everyone - even Samuel - was abandoning him. He must have been an emotional wreck, and he still faced a major battle.

Saul and his son Jonathan and the men with them were staying in Gibeah in Benjamin, while the Philistines camped at Mikmash. Raiding parties went out from the Philistine camp in three detachments. One turned toward Ophrah in the vicinity of Shual, another toward Beth Horon, and the third toward the borderland overlooking the Valley of Zeboyim facing the wilderness.

Not a blacksmith could be found in the whole land of Israel, because the Philistines had said, "Otherwise the Hebrews will make swords or spears!" So all Israel went down to the Philistines to have their plow points, mattocks, axes and sickles sharpened. The price was two-thirds of a shekel for sharpening plow points and mattocks, and a third of a shekel for sharpening forks and axes and for repointing goads.

So on the day of the battle not a soldier with Saul and Jonathan had a sword or spear in his hand; only Saul and his son Jonathan had them. (16-22)

We may think our government is incompetent, but this is amazing. The soldiers are ready to fight the Philistines, but they have no weapons. Crazy? Absolutely, but we do the same thing. We go into battle unarmed, figuring somehow we'll make it. Many go through life like that. Whether through lack of preparation or circumstances beyond your control, life is overwhelming. Of course God can mercifully intervene on your behalf, but your preparation may mean the difference between life and death. If you're prepared, even when your strength and resources are gone, you can make it. You cover yourself by anticipating unexpected battles, just like you have insurance for natural disasters. It's too late on the day of battle to run around trying to find weapons. I've lived through a couple hurricanes. Once the storm hits, it's too late to do much. You find out how well prepared you really are.

Obedience: The best preparation for victory in battle

Saul just lost his kingdom by disobeying a seemingly insignificant command about a sacrifice. The best strategy for victory in battle is developing a habit of scrupulous obedience. It's simplified, but the concept is scriptural:

- God wants you to win.

- He knows everything about the enemy and how to beat him.

- If you walk in obedience to him, he'll direct your steps to victory.

You can have all the weapons you want, but if you're not obeying God they won't do you any good. You can read all the books on spiritual warfare and know all the tactics to defeat the enemy, but if your life isn't in line with God's Word it's not going to help you much. Weapons are dangerous and ineffective in the hands of a soldier who's not following orders. In the army you go through basic training to learn obedience to your superiors. When they're confident you'll obey, they give you weapons and teach you how to use them. If you have a problem with obedience, start working there to prepare for battle.

Don't make agreements with the enemy

Did you notice the foolish arrangement Israel made? They had an unwritten agreement for the Philistines to do all their blacksmith work! The Philistines may have even placed agents in Israel to report anyone blacksmithing illegally! Saul didn't make the agreement, but as king he was responsible for following God's law, and he should have known how it grieved the Lord to enter into a contract with a heathen nation. *"When the Lord has delivered the nations over to you and you have defeated them, then you must destroy them totally. Make no treaty with them, and show them no mercy."[28]* That may sound harsh, but God always has a reason for his commands, even if it's not immediately obvious.

Many of us have unwritten agreements with the enemy; deals that appear beneficial. After all, the Philistines just wanted to help Israel because they didn't have all the necessary tools or skills. They'd even give them a discount. Don't buy it. They may be the nicest folks around. To imply they could be working for the devil sounds crazy. Good friendships probably developed between the Jews and their Philistine blacksmiths. After a while they forgot they worshiped another god and their leaders wanted them dead. It may take longer and cost more, but Israel should have refused the offer.

As Saul was learning, they were indeed the enemy. People in the world who seem like the nicest folks around can still be used by our enemy. Not to say they're demon possessed or you should have nothing to do with them, but if they're not part of the kingdom of God, Satan can deceive them and use them to accomplish his purposes, the principal of which is your destruction. When we try to get out of those agreements, Satan gets all over us. Remember Paul's command in II Corinthians 6 about being unequally yoked?[29]

What agreements have you made?

What are some of the deals, agreements, or partnerships you've made with the enemy? Here are a few common ones:

Marriage. In the closest relationship you can have, many enter into partnerships with unbelievers which pull you away from Christ and cause countless heartaches. This is an agreement you can't back out of. The Bible doesn't allow you to divorce because you mistakenly married an unbeliever.[30] If they choose to leave, you're released from that commitment, but otherwise you must live with the consequences of your decision.

Business deals. I met many men in prison because they made business deals with the enemy. Obviously, if you run a business, you can't deal exclusively with Christians, but when you make partnerships with unbelievers, you can expect problems.

Politics. Be careful about involvement with politics and the government. Are we making deals with the Philistines? Israel relied on her enemy for the basics of everyday life, supporting a nation dedicated to their destruction. Have we become too dependent on government handouts? Are we horrified at the thought of losing our tax deduction for charitable contributions?

Others have been trapped through drugs and alcohol, while many run to the Philistines for their entertainment and education. Israel's dependence became deadly. Where have you become dependent on the enemy? How can you break those agreements?

Know your enemy

Israel also showed an appalling ignorance of their enemy. They seemed fine with this cozy arrangement with the Philistine blacksmiths. They didn't think about all the money they were giving them or realize it was dangerous to have no way of making weapons.

Meanwhile, as is often the case, the enemy was smart, making sure Israel had to keep coming to them. It was obvious Israel wouldn't be much of a threat if they could be kept dependent. In battles today the world frequently outsmarts us. They know exactly what it takes to make people dependent on them, spending billions on advertising and extensive market research. And, just like Israel, we happily fill our minds with it and fail to see the trap. When the battle gets intense, we wonder why we're losing.

Be smart about your enemy. Don't get wrapped up in him or his world system. Examine how Satan has gotten people trapped in the past. Look at the world and observe his methods. Get to know his tactics so you can recognize the deal he's offering you - and refuse it.

Prepare your weapons

If you're a Christian, you will be involved in battle. Make sure your weapons are in order. What are they? *The weapons we fight with are not the weapons of the world. On the contrary, they have divine power to demolish strongholds.*[31] *We wrestle not against flesh and blood, but against principalities and powers and spiritual forces of wickedness in heavenly realms.*[32]

Some Christians load up on the world's weapons and fight like the world. In court, they use the legal system. In government, they use politics. If we're going to be involved in the courts or government, we need to make sure we're fighting with spiritual weapons.

Weapons of our warfare

There are many good books on spiritual warfare, but I want to touch on five of our weapons:

1. *Prayer.* How is your prayer life? Are you going to be caught unable to fight because you've never learned to use this weapon? Way beyond bringing requests to God, you need Spirit-directed warfare prayer. Are you praying regularly with other believers?

2. *The Word of God, the sword of the Spirit.* Just as Israel ran to the Philistines, many Christians run to the enemy for their sword. Their beliefs and world-view are formed more by the media and the world's brilliant thinkers than the Bible. You will lose the battle that way. A pretty sword hanging on your wall won't help you on the battlefield, and neither will a Bible sitting on your

shelf. How much of it is really in your heart? Get into the Word, and proclaim it as Jesus did when tempted by the enemy.

3. *Worship*. When you start worshiping God, the devil flees. Do you worship God privately? Do you enter into the worship at church - or find it boring? Is it just entertainment - a way to feel good? Are you taking advantage of every opportunity to worship God?

4. *Unity*. There's great power in brothers whose hearts are knit together. If the devil can divide us, he can defeat us. United prayer is particularly powerful.

5. *The spiritual armor in Ephesians 6*. Just as you wouldn't leave home in your underwear, don't start the day without putting on your spiritual armor.

Saul did one more thing which was inexcusable. He and his son Jonathan were armed, but he neglected to arm his troops. If you're a pastor, that's your responsibility. Don't fall into Saul's sin of being ready for battle yourself but not equipping the believers in your care.

Now is the time to begin preparing for battle. Where have you made agreements and deals with the enemy? Break those agreements and trust God to provide for you. Get your weapons ready. You have an enemy who wants to destroy you.

Chapter 10

A True Man of God:
1 Samuel 14:1-23

Six hundred terrified, unarmed soldiers are hiding in caves. Their king is falling apart. Thousands of well-equipped Philistine soldiers are approaching. Defeat is guaranteed, right?

Wrong. We're talking about God's people. Even in the most desperate situation there's a "but" with God - an opportunity for him to do the impossible. The man he uses here is the kind of man God needs today - and it just so happens to be Saul's son, the same one who started this trouble by raiding a Philistine outpost.

One day Jonathan son of Saul said to his young armor-bearer, "Come, let's go over to the Philistine outpost on the other side." But he did not tell his father.

Saul was staying on the outskirts of Gibeah under a pomegranate tree in Migron. With him were about six hundred men, among whom was Ahijah, who was wearing an ephod. He was a son of Ichabod's brother Ahitub son of Phinehas, the son of Eli, the Lord's priest in Shiloh. No one was aware that Jonathan had left.

On each side of the pass that Jonathan intended to cross to reach the Philistine outpost was a cliff; one was called Bozez and the other Seneh. One cliff stood to the north toward Mikmash, the other to the south toward Geba.

Jonathan said to his young armor-bearer, "Come, let's go over to the outpost of those uncircumcised men. Perhaps the Lord will act in our behalf. Nothing can hinder the Lord from saving, whether by many or by few."

"Do all that you have in mind," his armor-bearer said. "Go ahead; I am with you heart and soul."

Jonathan said, "Come on, then; we will cross over toward them and let them see us. If they say to us, 'Wait there until we come to you,' we will stay where we are and not go up to them. But if they say, 'Come up to us,' we will climb up, because that will be our sign that the Lord has given them into our hands."

So both of them showed themselves to the Philistine outpost. "Look!" said the Philistines. "The Hebrews are crawling out of the holes they were hiding in." The men of the outpost shouted to Jonathan and his armor-bearer, "Come up to us and we'll teach you a lesson." So Jonathan said to his armor-bearer, "Climb up after me; the Lord has given them into the hand of Israel."

Jonathan climbed up, using his hands and feet, with his armor-bearer right behind him. The Philistines fell before Jonathan, and his armor-bearer followed and killed behind him. In that first attack Jonathan and his armor-bearer killed some twenty men in an area of about half an acre. (1-14)

I like Jonathan. I can relate to him. I'd call him a "man's man." Wouldn't you like to spend time with him?

Jonathan was a bold man

What a contrast to the Israelite army hiding and taking off across the Jordan, paralyzed by fear in the face of impossible odds. Jonathan watched them and knew they were not about to confront the enemy, so he did. He sees the need and his father's failure to respond, and decides to act. There's good reason *he did not tell his father.* Jonathan knew Saul would forbid him to go. Not only is Saul a coward, he also keeps others from moving out in faith. When bold men want to act, cowards try to stop them with their logical arguments.

Years ago when I read about D-day (a key World War II battle), I was overwhelmed with emotion. Sadness at the incredible loss of life, but also envy. That day there was a courage and boldness we rarely see anymore. Were those soldiers scared? Sure! But there were bold leaders willing to do what was necessary to turn the tide of the war.

Our nation is crippled by lack of boldness (could we call it cowardice?) at a time when we need bold leadership to face challenges in the family, church, and government. The enemy's been successful in robbing us of our masculinity, making us weak, fearful, and ineffective. God designed you to take the initiative and impact your world as you step out in holy boldness - an essential quality of the man of God.

- Boldness is defined as having courage, being fearless.

- Three times God instructs Joshua to be bold and courageous.[33]

- God *made* David bold and stouthearted.[34]

- *"The wicked man flees though no one is pursuing, but the righteous are as* bold *as a lion."* [35]

- *"A wicked man puts up a* bold *front, but an upright man gives thought to his ways."* [36] There can be a rash show of boldness which is a poor imitation of the real thing.

- The believers in Acts 4 pray God would enable them to speak the word with great boldness.

How can you become bold? Seek God. The more you reflect God's image, the bolder you'll become.

The world pictures the bold man as a beer-drinking, cigarette-smoking, macho man who does his own thing, trampling everyone around him. Jonathan was a man of boldness – but it was harnessed boldness.

Jonathan was a man of faith

Maybe he became such close friends with David because his heart beat with God's heart: *"Come, let's go over to the outpost of those uncircumcised fellows. Perhaps the Lord will act on our behalf. Nothing can hinder the Lord from saving, whether by many or by few."* God's reputation was at stake, and he knew God wants to reveal his saving power.

Faith is demonstrated by stepping out into a place where God can use you, where faith combines with holy boldness. Faith is willing to be vulnerable and take risks while believing that God will use and protect you. Lack of faith can keep you from speaking to your neighbor about Christ or praying for someone's healing – in case they don't get healed and you look stupid.

Faith is seeing things from God's perspective: *"Nothing can hinder the Lord from saving, whether by many or by few."* Do you have that kind of faith for the salvation of your family? Can you say with Jeremiah *"Ah, Lord God, you have made the heavens and the earth by your outstretched arm. Nothing is too difficult for you."*?[37] Or do you only see the obstacles? Faith is aware of them – but also aware of a much greater God. Faith has a clear understanding of whom we are in Christ – and who our enemy is. Faith gives confidence that God is with us.

Faith also includes looking to God and trusting him for guidance. Don't tempt God. I don't recommend setting things up as Jonathan did, but faith is confident God won't put you out on a limb without showing you how to get down. Jonathan made himself available to God, trusting him to act - if that was his will. He also believed God would protect him if it wasn't. What Jonathan did was very different from the presumption that passes as faith today. He didn't go out "claiming" victory and demanding that God do what he wanted him to do. Faith submits to God and confidently expects him to show the way. When God confirmed his direction, Jonathan was ready to move.

God is seeking men who combine boldness with faith, who see challenges and battlegrounds as opportunities for him to work. God is able to use just one man who is sold out to him, whose masculine passion is directed by a dynamic relationship with his Creator. We need to get away from the "bigger is better" mentality. It only takes mustard seed faith for him to move mountains. One man who is bold and ready to step out in faith can change the world. But to do that, there are two more essential qualities.

Jonathan knew how to build meaningful relationships

Bold men may be rugged individualists, and men of faith often struggle in relationships, but close friendships are part of God's design for manhood. The man of God - like Jonathan - knows how to share his heart and life with others. He reached out to other men - and they responded. He'd already picked an armor-bearer, and now they set off on this adventure. But it was more than just a working relationship. The armor-bearer says *"I am with you heart and soul."* Would you like someone to say that to you? Have you ever had that kind of friend?

True masculinity like Jonathan's attracts others - women, but also other men. Those deep relationships foster boldness. A man of God shares his heart and elicits commitment: *"I am with you heart and soul."* It's not about lone rangers - God will impact our world through men whose hearts are knit together.

Jonathan's motive was God's glory

A man of God is concerned about God's name and glory. The man seeking his own glory won't make it far with God.

Men with all four qualities are few and far between. Out of all the armies of Israel, Jonathan appears to be the only "real man." Don't be surprised if you can't find many like him. Sin has left a deep mark on us. But when you find one, draw close to him, work with him, support him, and learn from him.

This experience isn't beyond your reach. God made you a man, and he wants you to come alive as a man. You probably won't look like Jonathan, but get in touch with your own masculinity and let the strength of a Jonathan encourage you.

Where's Saul?

Jonathan saved Israel that day in spite of Saul. What a contrast between the father and the godly masculinity of his son!

Saul was staying on the outskirts of Gibeah under a pomegranate tree in Migron. With him were about six hundred men, among whom was Ahijah, who was wearing an ephod. He was a son of Ichabod's brother Ahitub son of Phinehas, the son of Eli, the Lord's priest in Shiloh. No one was aware that Jonathan had left. (2-3)

Then panic struck the whole army—those in the camp and field, and those in the outposts and raiding parties—and the ground shook. It was a panic sent by God. Saul's lookouts at Gibeah in Benjamin saw the army melting away in all directions. Then Saul said to the men who were with him, "Muster the forces and see who has left us." When they did, it was Jonathan and his armor-bearer who were not there.

Saul said to Ahijah, "Bring the ark of God." (At that time it was with the Israelites.) While Saul was talking to the priest, the tumult in the Philistine camp increased more and more. So Saul said to the priest, "Withdraw your hand."

Then Saul and all his men assembled and went to the battle. They found the Philistines in total confusion, striking each other with their swords. Those Hebrews who had previously been with the Philistines and had gone up with them to their camp went over to the Israelites who were with Saul and Jonathan. When all the Israelites who had hidden in the hill country of Ephraim heard that the Philistines were on the run, they joined the battle in hot pursuit. So on that day the Lord saved Israel, and the battle moved on beyond Beth Aven. (15-23)

Jonathan was boldly moving out in faith. And Saul? Hanging out under a pomegranate tree! What was he doing there when his army was about to be devastated?

Saul is disengaged from his world

A lot of men are hanging out under pomegranate trees instead of moving powerfully into their world. The enemy is coming against their marriage, family, church, and nation - and they're at home on the internet or watching TV. They're paralyzed, wasting their lives, and withdrawn from their wives, families, and friends. It's a real temptation. Resist it! If you've fallen prey, repent, get up, and get moving. Look for a Jonathan to do battle with.

Saul had a twisted religion

There are two completely different stories being told here. It's no accident *no one was aware that Jonathan had left.* They were in such different worlds they weren't even aware of what he was doing. God was on the battlefield, with Jonathan and his armor bearer, sending panic on the Philistines and rescuing Israel. Saul watched the action from a distance, trying to find an explanation for what God was doing and looking to see who'd left his camp – as if he couldn't believe one of his men was causing this.

He was surrounded by "religious" men who were part of the institutionalized priesthood. Ahijah was wearing an ephod, a priestly garment. The priests with him were Eli's wicked grandsons. For good measure Saul called for the ark. The tumult in the Philistine camp was getting greater, and Saul was wasting precious time, too busy being religious to get involved in what God was doing. He was getting ready while God was already fighting the battle.

Many men today are holed up in churches debating what's happening, lost in dead religion, while God is at work all around them. They're trying to find the proper theological explanation, while God is defeating the enemy. They fondly remember the "glory days" of the American church, while God is moving in Africa, Asia, and Latin America. They endlessly prepare for battle, when God has already given them the victory if they'd just get out there and do something.

Saul is the perfect example of the emasculated male. Do you want to be out of touch with your masculinity? Follow his path of disobedience and use religion for what you can get out of it. Focus on yourself and your reputation, how you look, and your abilities or lack thereof. In some ways it's the easier path - but far less rewarding.

The differences between father and son are amazing. It's encouraging to know you can have a messed up dad like Saul and still come out okay! Or be a messed up father like Saul and have a son who comes out okay! Our souls long to be like Jonathan: a man of boldness, faith, and relationship, who impacts his world and moves out in power and strength for God's glory. It's not something you can work up. Contrary to what many think, it comes from being in relationship with the ultimate man's man - Jesus. The more his image is restored in you, the more alive you'll feel as a man. What kind of man do you want to be?

Chapter 11

False Machismo:
1 Samuel 14:24-52

Full of God's Spirit, Jonathan courageously attacked the enemy. His father, spiritually empty, was sitting under a pomegranate tree, out of touch with reality and facing disaster. Men who are out of control often put on a show of macho bravado.

Now the Israelites were in distress that day, because Saul had bound the people under an oath, saying, "Cursed be anyone who eats food before evening comes, before I have avenged myself on my enemies!" So none of the troops tasted food. (24)

A foolish oath

Saul obviously wasn't responsible for Jonathan's victory, but somehow it empowered him and left him wanting more, so he foolishly bound his men with this oath. God may call a fast, but this had nothing to do with God, and it certainly wasn't typical battle strategy. It was all about Saul. The troops couldn't eat *"before I have avenged **myself** on my enemies."* The battle with the Philistines had become personal. After so many failures, Saul was determined to prove himself. After all, he was still king! He'd show his strength by fasting and forcing his troops to fast, with no concern for their well-being.

The foolishness of his decision is revealed in its fruit. The men were faint with hunger, in distress, and afraid of the oath. Was that any way to fight a battle? Wouldn't it make sense to have the troops well fed? Wouldn't you want them feeling good and confident, instead of under the threat of some curse?

While Saul withheld food, God miraculously provided it: *The entire army entered the woods, and there was honey on the ground. When they went into the woods, they saw the honey oozing out; yet no one put his hand to his mouth, because they feared the oath.* (25-26)

Imagine starving, seeing all this delicious honey, and not being able to touch it! Leaders on ego trips, like Saul, hurt the people they're supposed to be caring for, masking their weakness by grabbing whatever power and control they can get. They're not thinking straight, so things can get ugly and scary, as only too many women and children know. Maybe you've suffered under an insecure boss.

Jonathan breaks the oath

While dad's making a fool of himself, what's our man Jonathan up to?

But Jonathan had not heard that his father had bound the people with the oath, so he reached out the end of the staff that was in his hand and dipped it into the honeycomb. He raised his hand to his mouth, and his eyes brightened. Then one of the soldiers told him, "Your father bound the army under a strict oath, saying, 'Cursed be anyone who eats food today!' That is why the men are faint."

Jonathan said, "My father has made trouble for the country. See how my eyes brightened when I tasted a little of this honey. How much better it would have been if the men had eaten today some of the plunder they took from their enemies. Would not the slaughter of the Philistines have been even greater?" (27-30)

I can't help but think God purposely arranged this, and was probably chuckling. Jonathan had been out fighting, so he didn't know about the prohibition. He saw the honey, ate it, and was immediately revived. The troops probably already knew it, but Jonathan was bold enough to say it: his father wasn't considering what was best for his men or the nation. If they hadn't been famished, the victory would have been much greater. Was Jonathan dishonoring his father and his king? He was never rebuked for what he did. How far do we go in honoring our parents or someone in authority? If they're in sin, are we required to do what they say? Or is part of honor telling them the truth?

Meanwhile, things were rapidly spiraling out of control with the famished army.

That day, after the Israelites had struck down the Philistines from Mikmash to Aijalon, they were exhausted. They pounced on the plunder and, taking sheep, cattle and calves, they butchered them on the ground and ate them, together with the blood.

Then someone said to Saul, "Look, the men are sinning against the Lord by eating meat that has blood in it."
"You have broken faith," he said. "Roll a large stone over here at once." Then he said, "Go out among the men and tell them, 'Each of you bring me your cattle and sheep, and slaughter them here and eat them. Do not sin against the Lord by eating meat with blood still in it.'"

So everyone brought his ox that night and slaughtered it there. Then Saul built an altar to the Lord; it was the first time he had done this.

Saul said, "Let us go down and pursue the Philistines by night and plunder them till dawn, and let us not leave one of them alive." "Do whatever seems best to you," they replied. But the priest said, "Let us inquire of God here." So Saul asked God, "Shall I go down and pursue the Philistines? Will you give them into Israel's hand?" But God did not answer him that day. (31-37)

Saul comes to the rescue

Something's wrong. God's not speaking, and Saul's alarmed. Because the men obeyed his crazy rule, they end up breaking the law that really mattered, and sinning against God. It would never have happened if they'd been allowed to eat. When you devote your energy to burdensome man-made rules and remove legitimate pleasure from your life, you risk more serious temptations. Beware of rules that sound spiritual, but are based on pride instead of Scripture.

Just days before, Saul had been severely disciplined for disobedience. Now he comes to the rescue as the great defender of the law. To reinforce his image as a spiritual giant he builds an altar to the Lord giving thanks for the victory. It sounds good, but pay attention to subtle messages the writers put in Scripture. A few words can say a whole lot. This was the *first* altar Saul built. What happened after his great victory back in chapter eleven? Didn't he build an altar when he was anointed king? Or an altar of repentance when God judged him? Why did he wait until now? Had he experienced a spiritual awakening? Was he really thanking God?

Saul tasted blood, and wants more. He's on a roll, and he wants to make sure God's with him. Just like the earlier fast, an altar seems like the right thing to do, even though he had no intention of seeking God there. He'd already made his plans. The priest has to suggest consulting the Lord before this major battle. Saul appears to have no relationship with God, so it's not too surprising that when he finally does pray, there's no answer. Yet somehow he knew it was sin blocking God's response:

Saul therefore said, "Come here, all you who are leaders of the army, and let us find out what sin has been committed today. As surely as the Lord who rescues Israel lives, even if the guilt lies with my son Jonathan, he must die." But not one of them said a word.

Saul then said to all the Israelites, "You stand over there; I and Jonathan my son will stand over here."

"Do what seems best to you," they replied.

Then Saul prayed to the Lord, the God of Israel, "Why have you not answered your servant today? If the fault is in me or my son Jonathan, respond with Urim, but if the men of Israel are at fault, respond with Thummim." Jonathan and Saul were taken by lot, and the men were cleared. Saul said, "Cast the lot between me and Jonathan my son." And Jonathan was taken. (38-42)

You'd think he might have learned the first time, but he perpetuates the appearance of strength with another foolish oath. Saul doesn't know his son broke the first oath, but the men do. They weren't about to give Jonathan up, but God does, by answering Saul's prayer. I've never been quite sure why God honored the casting of lots, but he often did, and this time the lot fell to Jonathan.

Then Saul said to Jonathan, "Tell me what you have done."
So Jonathan told him, "I tasted a little honey with the end of my staff. And now I must die!"

Saul said, "May God deal with me, be it ever so severely, if you do not die, Jonathan."

But the men said to Saul, "Should Jonathan die—he who has brought about this great deliverance in Israel? Never! As surely as the Lord lives, not a hair of his head will fall to the ground, for he did this today with God's help." So the men rescued Jonathan, and he was not put to death.

Then Saul stopped pursuing the Philistines, and they withdrew to their own land. (43-46)

Look how far Saul has fallen! To save face and look tough he would kill his own son for unknowingly violating his father's foolish command. Saul was ready to sacrifice his family to his pride.

Have you known fathers jealous of their son's success? Maybe your dad? Or you? It's not uncommon. Saul was so wrapped up in himself he was ready to kill Jonathan for his success and virility instead of rejoicing in it, but his men had put up with enough and would mutiny before allowing it. Saul was forced to back down and Jonathan's life was spared, but instead of acknowledging his poor decisions and retreating gracefully, he stood firm until he looked like an idiot and lost the army's respect. It did impact Saul, though. Gone were his big plans of killing every single Philistine. They went home very much alive. If he'd been wiser, they might have been defeated once and for all, but now he'll experience bitter warfare with them for the rest of his life.

A big show of machismo isn't real strength and it doesn't fool anybody. It's obnoxious and makes you look bad. Don't build altars for appearance sake or let your pride and personal problems harm your relationship to your family. Don't get caught up in legalism which supposedly demonstrates your strength and spirituality. Be careful of the declarations you make. I've heard pastors declare many things in a moment of spiritual fervor, only to be embarrassed later on when they didn't happen. They sound impressive, but may have nothing to do with God. Be real, and don't be afraid to acknowledge your mistakes.

Amazingly, the chapter finishes on a positive note:

After Saul had assumed rule over Israel, he fought against their enemies on every side: Moab, the Ammonites, Edom, the kings of Zobah, and the Philistines. Wherever he turned, he inflicted punishment on them. He fought valiantly and defeated the Amalekites, delivering Israel from the hands of those who had plundered them.

All the days of Saul there was bitter war with the Philistines, and whenever Saul saw a mighty or brave man, he took him into his service. (47-48, 52)

Somehow Saul became a valiant fighter. He was able to spot mighty and brave men and draw them into his service, even though he was not particularly brave or mighty. Saul reigned for many more years. Perhaps he learned from his mistakes and finally got it together?

Chapter 12

One Last Chance to Redeem Himself:
1 Samuel 15:1-35

Aren't you glad God doesn't give up on you? He gives Saul a chance to redeem himself, sending Samuel with a new assignment. This could be a turning point for the struggling king.

Samuel said to Saul, "I am the one the Lord sent to anoint you king over his people Israel; so listen now to the message from the Lord." (1)

That's an odd way for a spiritual father to greet his son. Had Saul forgotten who Samuel was? Since Samuel started Saul on the journey, he's probably emphasizing the importance of this assignment.

This is what the Lord Almighty says: 'I will punish the Amalekites for what they did to Israel when they waylaid them as they came up from Egypt. Now go, attack the Amalekites and totally destroy all that belongs to them. Do not spare them; put to death men and women, children and infants, cattle and sheep, camels and donkeys.'" (2-3)

The assignment

This has been on God's heart a long time. The Amalekites attacked Israel on their way up from Egypt.[38] That day God said

91

"I will completely blot out the memory of Amalek from under heaven," and Moses added *"The Lord will be at war against the Amalekites from generation to generation."* Many years passed and God had done nothing. If the Amalekites knew what God said they may have decided it was an empty threat. But God doesn't forget. He'd just been waiting for the right time and the right man. It seems like a sure win for Saul. He knows exactly what to do, and God will surely grant him success.

Do you ever cry out to God like the Psalmist, "How long, Oh Lord?"[39] You may be tempted to take things into your own hands and fight those who have wronged you or the Lord. At times God seems slow to keep his promises, but he knows what he's doing. When he wants you to do something, he'll let you know. Has he given you an assignment? Maybe a make or break task like Saul's? Is he testing you? Are you in a battle right now? Is it of your own making, or has God sent you? If you're on a mission from God, he'll be with you!

Saul totally destroys the Amalekites!

So Saul summoned the men and mustered them at Telaim - two hundred thousand foot soldiers and ten thousand from Judah. Saul went to the city of Amalek and set an ambush in the ravine. Then he said to the Kenites, "Go away, leave the Amalekites so that I do not destroy you along with them; for you showed kindness to all the Israelites when they came up out of Egypt." So the Kenites moved away from the Amalekites. Then Saul attacked the Amalekites all the way from Havilah to Shur, near the eastern border of Egypt. He took Agag king of the Amalekites alive, and all his people he totally destroyed with the sword. (4-8)

What a great start! Saul's well prepared this time, with an impressive army of 210,000 soldiers. He thoughtfully warned any foreigners to get out, since he's determined to kill everything. The king is captured and all the people destroyed. He's learned from his mistakes! Saul's finally getting it right!

But . . . suddenly the scene changes. That "but" in obedience can prove disastrous.

The "but" that destroyed Saul

But Saul and the army spared Agag and the best of the sheep and cattle, the fat calves and lambs—everything that was good. These they were unwilling to destroy completely, but everything that was despised and weak they totally destroyed. (9)

What are they thinking? Did they forget what God said? They do what makes sense to them - destroying what's weak and despised, but sparing what's good.

> *"Those poor lambs. They're perfect specimens. We just can't destroy them. Besides, we can sacrifice them to God!"*

We apply our reasoning to God's word. We make a point of getting rid of the weak and despised things - and feel good about it. But we hold on to what the world says is good, and disobey God. Saul should have stepped forward to enforce God's command, but he's right there with the army in their sin.

This wasn't the first time Israel disobeyed God's order to destroy everything. Saul had to know how Acan brought defeat to the nation after the walls of Jericho fell.[40] And Israel was plagued for centuries by people they failed to destroy when they entered the promised land. God commands us to destroy every enemy in our lives, but we usually don't, and end up battling them for years. Are there any "sacred cows" you're holding onto?

Samuel confronts Saul

Then the word of the Lord came to Samuel: "I regret (grieve) that I have made Saul king, because he has turned away from me and has not carried out my instructions." Samuel was troubled and angry, and he cried out to the Lord all that night. (10-11)

Just when it seemed Saul might get it together, he disobeys and turns away from the Lord, all about himself and his own importance. Was Samuel angry with Saul, or with himself? Or with God - for rejecting Saul? Was he feeling God's anger and grief over Saul's rebellion, or troubled by the whole ugly scene? Probably all of it! He'd been with Saul from the beginning and had seen his failures, but he still couldn't give up on him. I pray God would never have to grieve over your disobedience or failure to live up to your potential and calling. That's tragic - and scary, if you have any fear of God. Samuel knew God's heart, and spent a sleepless night calling out to him. Are you willing to give up a night's sleep to intercede for someone in rebellion?

A monument in his own honor

Early in the morning Samuel got up and went to meet Saul, but he was told, "Saul has gone to Carmel. There he has set up a monument in his own honor and has turned and gone on down to Gilgal." (12)

After his victory in I Samuel 14 Saul had built an altar to the Lord, but now we see where his heart's really at. While God was grieving over his sin and disobedience, he'd gone to erect a monument *in his own honor*! Apparently he was so out of touch with the Lord he could disobey direct orders and think he was doing great. Do we build monuments in our own honor? A college? A new wing on the church? A ministry? May God deliver us from such arrogance!

Finally, tired and burdened, Samuel catches up with Saul, who proudly comes out to greet him.

When Samuel reached him, Saul said, "The Lord bless you! I have carried out the Lord's instructions." (13)

Was he lying, or so deceived he really thought he'd done everything right? I've known many Christians wrapped up in themselves and blind to reality, sure they were God's man for the hour. It's possible Saul was that deceived, but God has a way of allowing reality catch up with us.

Bleating sheep and lowing cattle

But Samuel said, "What then is this bleating of sheep in my ears? What is this lowing of cattle that I hear?"

Saul answered, "The soldiers brought them from the Amalekites; they spared the best of the sheep and cattle to sacrifice to the Lord your God, but we totally destroyed the rest." (14-15)

There was only one small problem with Saul's story. Bleating sheep and lowing cattle. Wasn't Saul supposed to destroy them? He had the perfect excuse, and it's even spiritual: They were going to sacrifice them! Saul actually may have felt this would please God. I can picture many Christians buying the story. It sounds good, if you don't take God's word seriously and think you have room to modify his commands for your own convenience. But it's too much for Samuel.

"Enough!" Samuel said to Saul. "Let me tell you what the Lord said to me last night."

"Tell me," Saul replied.

Samuel said, "Although you were once small in your own eyes, did you not become the head of the tribes of Israel? The Lord anointed you king over Israel. And he sent you on a mission, saying, 'Go and completely destroy those wicked people, the Amalekites; wage war against them until you have wiped them out.' Why did you not obey the Lord? Why did you pounce on the plunder and do evil in the eyes of the Lord?" (16-19)

Saul began with a poor self-image, but now his ego was inflated. He'd forgotten what God had done in his life, and when God isn't at the center we tend to swing between those two extremes. Most important, he had disobeyed God's clear command. It's easy to condemn Saul, but we too can quickly forget our broken, sinful, past and God's deliverance. We disobey God, and then look down on those still lost in their sin.

"But I did obey the Lord," Saul said. "I went on the mission the Lord assigned me. I completely destroyed the Amalekites and brought back Agag their king. The soldiers took sheep and cattle from the plunder, the best of what was devoted to God, in order to sacrifice them to the Lord your God at Gilgal." (20-21)

Passing the blame is as old as Adam. Saul won't acknowledge his responsibility as leader: *"I completely destroyed the Amalekites"*, but *"**the soldiers** took the sheep and cattle."* And was it just a slip of the tongue when Saul called the Lord *your* God when he spoke to Samuel? Is it possible God was no longer Saul's Lord - or never had been?

100% obedience required

Saul may have completed 95% of what God wanted - and thought he was doing great. Many Christians today would agree. But God isn't interested in 95% obedience. He requires 100%. When we fail, he's merciful - if we're honest and come to him in genuine repentance and humility. God knows we're human and make mistakes, even though some people (especially bosses!) may feel they're infallible. If you fall into sin, don't try to cover or excuse it, as Saul did: *"But I did obey!"* Be real, and honest, and humble enough to acknowledge what you've done. Samuel's not impressed with Saul's excuse, and neither is God.

Obedience vs. religion

But Samuel replied:
"Does the Lord delight in burnt offerings and sacrifices
as much as in obeying the Lord?
To obey is better than sacrifice,
and to heed is better than the fat of rams.

For rebellion is like the sin of divination,
and arrogance like the evil of idolatry.
Because you have rejected the word of the Lord,
he has rejected you as king." (22-23)

Do you want to please God? Obey him. That message has come through repeatedly in this book. To obey you have to hear God's voice and know what he wants you to do. Don't pick out what you feel like doing - and ignore parts of the Bible you don't agree with! Don't be like Saul, setting yourself up as a judge of God's Word. We often destroy the weak and despised things of our culture while trying to salvage the fat of the land to use in service to God. Be careful of rejecting the Lord's Word by your actions!

God says that rebellion is like divination or witchcraft, and arrogance is idolatry. Saul might have been shocked to hear that, as most Christians would be. Rebellion and arrogance were big problems for Saul, and they are for many of us. All those animals Saul was going to sacrifice meant absolutely nothing to the Lord if he wasn't walking in obedience. To obey is better than sacrifice. All our worship services and fancy churches grieve God's heart if we're not listening to his word and obeying it.

Saul's fatal flaw

Then Saul said to Samuel, "I have sinned. I violated the Lord's command and your instructions. I was afraid of the men and so I gave in to them. Now I beg you, forgive my sin and come back with me, so that I may worship the Lord."

But Samuel said to him, "I will not go back with you. You have rejected the word of the Lord, and the Lord has rejected you as king over Israel!"

As Samuel turned to leave, Saul caught hold of the hem of his robe, and it tore. Samuel said to him, "The Lord has torn the kingdom of Israel from you today and has given it to one of your neighbors—to one better than you. He who is the Glory of Israel does not lie or change his mind; for he is not a human being, that he should change his mind."

Saul replied, "I have sinned. But please honor me before the elders of my people and before Israel; come back with me, so that I may worship the Lord your God." So Samuel went back with Saul, and Saul worshiped the Lord. (24-31)

It's sad, but it often takes some disaster, like seeing your wife walk out, or being arrested, to get your attention. When Saul heard the consequences of his sin, his confession revealed a fatal flaw: *"I was afraid of the men and so I gave in to them."*

It may be that Saul set out to do the right thing, but was weak and afraid of his own men. The soldiers brought the animals and he didn't have the strength to command their slaughter. His inner weakness and failure to stand up for what's right caused his downfall. If you're afraid of men, you're not fit for Christian leadership. If you can be influenced to reject the word of God to please men, you will be rejected by God.

How sincere was Saul? In these situations many repent in hopes of avoiding sin's consequences. It's not genuine. Why was Saul so intent on worshiping? Was there a part of him that sought God and got something from worship? I've seen enough troubled men honestly desire to worship God that I can't write him off. Saul may have had some spiritual hunger - but there was too much inner confusion for him to get things right with God. He wanted to worship the Lord - but wanted Samuel to come with him *to honor him* [Saul] *before the elders and people of Israel.* It seems to be more about looking good before the people than about God. If it appeared Samuel wasn't with him, they'd look down on him. Samuel saw right through it and wanted nothing to do with his phony worship. In desperation Saul grabbed Samuel's robe - and tore it. Finally Samuel agreed to go and worship with him.

Before Samuel left there was one more thing to do. Saul hadn't put the Amalekite king to death, so the aged prophet would have to.

Then Samuel said, "Bring me Agag king of the Amalekites." Agag came to him in chains. And he thought, "Surely the bitterness of death is past." But Samuel said, "As your sword has made women childless,
so will your mother be childless among women." And Samuel put Agag to death before the Lord at Gilgal.

Then Samuel left for Ramah, but Saul went up to his home in Gibeah of Saul. Until the day Samuel died, he did not go to see Saul again, though Samuel mourned for him. And the Lord regretted that he had made Saul king over Israel. (32-35)

It's good to know you're not the only one with regrets.

Lessons for spiritual fathers

Samuel was not a "hovering" father. He spent time with Saul and then let him go and try out what he'd been taught.

- He based his input into Saul's life on God's word, not his own thoughts about what he should be doing.

- He didn't let his failure with his own sons intimidate him into backing off from Saul. Indeed, his own failures may have motivated and helped him father Saul.

- Samuel didn't excuse Saul's disobedience or attempt to minimize its seriousness. He wasn't afraid to confront Saul with the truth. It's possible to get so attached to someone you don't want to do anything to jeopardize that relationship. Be careful if you feel that way.

Samuel grieved for Saul the rest of his life. You may understand how he felt. It could be your own son, or someone you've mentored. You cannot and should not control what he does. He will make mistakes. Hopefully he'll learn from them - but he may not. If you've invested in him and love him, it will hurt to see him fall, just like it hurts to see your own children fall.

Samuel did what God told him to do. Saul was God's choice as king. The fact that Saul ultimately failed was not Samuel's fault. While Samuel might have considered himself a failure, he'd been faithful. You can't take responsibility for your spiritual son's failure . . . or success. Thank God for the opportunity to speak into his life, to love him, and to stick with him through thick and thin, as Samuel did with Saul. Where would Saul have been without Samuel? Probably back on the farm plowing with his oxen.

When Saul realized things were almost over he desperately grabbed for Samuel's robe. The point had arrived, however, when their relationship effectively ended. There may be times when those mentoring relationships need to end. I suspect if Saul had reached out to Samuel he would have been there, although it never happened. I am confident that Samuel continued to pray as he grieved over him.

Avoid Saul's downfall

How easy to fool ourselves into thinking we're obeying God when we're only selectively obedient. God is more concerned about obedience than religion. We hope that with a few "sacrifices" or religious rituals we can please him. How's your obedience? Ninety per cent? Fifty per cent? God forgives your sin, but he still requires 100%. How dare we claim to know better than God what's best! How dare we decide what to accept and reject in his word! Be careful of the trap Saul found himself in! He thought he'd done everything right, when actually he was deep in sin. It's chillingly reminiscent of the ones Jesus judges in Matthew.[41] Do whatever it takes to deal with your rebellion and arrogance. God will help you avoid these traps as he breaks you and humbles you.

PART THREE

I t's time to face the consequences of your earlier choices. This is autumn, or the twilight of your life. God's charge and equipping to reign hasn't changed, but the condition God places on it becomes more urgent: *If we endure, we will also reign with him.*[42]

If you've endured and continued to walk with God, you'll experience the fullness of the authority he intends for you, and be ready for an eternity of reigning with Christ. Your faith is solid. You're enjoying friendships with your children, who have their own families and careers. Grandchildren are a joy. You've worked through problems in your marriage and have a mature love and better sexual intimacy than ever. You've watched your budget and invested wisely, allowing you to give freely and live comfortably. You're a respected, contributing member of your church and community. Even though you can tell there's some mileage on your body - you might need some meds or even minor surgery - you've watched your diet and exercise, and you're in good shape. You have wisdom and contentment you didn't know as a young man, and life feels full and rich.

But it's also possible your poor choices have caught up with you, and life is a battle ruled by fear, failure, and circumstances. You never took the time to get into God's Word and develop your relationship with him, and now your faith feels empty. You alienated your children, who have their own lives and no time for you. Your marriage couldn't take the neglect and abuse, and you're divorced and lonely. You wasted money and didn't save for retirement, so you have to keep working and wonder how you're going to make it. You've abused your body and are plagued with diabetes, heart disease, or cancer. Any activity becomes a chore. Too many burned bridges have left you isolated in your community.

Most of us will probably fall somewhere between these two extremes. If you haven't reached this journey yet, let them serve as a solemn reminder to follow God and make the right choices. If you're an older man, you probably have your share of regrets, disappointments, and broken dreams. By this point it's hard to correct the mistakes you've made, but you have experience and wisdom younger men lack. You can accept where you're at and choose to make the most of the rest of your life. It's not too late to repent and let God change you. There's still hope!

Chapter 13

Saul and David:
1 Samuel 16:1-23

This chapter marks the turning point of I Samuel, as the focus moves from Saul to his replacement, a young man after God's own heart. Saul is already on his way down and out, even though it will be years before he takes his own life.

One more task for Samuel

Samuel continued to play a key role in Saul's life after his official farewell. Even when God rejected Saul it was hard for Samuel to let go of him, but God's work goes on, and we need to move on with him and stop mourning the person who rejects him.

The Lord said to Samuel, "How long will you mourn for Saul, since I have rejected him as king over Israel? Fill your horn with oil and be on your way; I am sending you to Jesse of Bethlehem. I have chosen one of his sons to be king."

But Samuel said, "How can I go? If Saul hears about it, he will kill me."
The Lord said, "Take a heifer with you and say, 'I have come to sacrifice to the Lord.' (1-2)

Bizarre as it sounds, God agrees that Samuel had good reason to fear for his life! The depraved mind that rejects God is capable of incredible evil. God actually suggests bending the truth with a cover!

Men look at the outward appearance, but the Lord looks at the heart

When they arrived, Samuel saw Eliab and thought, "Surely the Lord's anointed stands here before the Lord."

But the Lord said to Samuel, "Do not consider his appearance or his height, for I have rejected him. The Lord does not look at the things people look at. People look at the outward appearance, but the Lord looks at the heart." (6-7)

Even after all those years, Samuel didn't get it. I find it encouraging that a great prophet still had things to learn. It wasn't about what made sense to him; his job was to hear from God. If he wasn't listening, he could have anointed the wrong man. No matter how experienced you are, you can still blow it if you rely on your own wisdom. You need to hear from God – today.

Samuel figured if God chose Saul because he was tall and handsome, he'd choose Eliab, who was also tall and handsome. But Saul's looks had never been important to God. He's not concerned with outward appearances. He looks at the heart. The world values the handsome man or beautiful woman, and we tend to do the same. Are you impressed with those who *look* the most spiritual? They may not be. Someone struggling through trials may have a heart that's right with God. Don't be swayed by appearances. Try to discern where the heart's at. Do you spend as much time looking at your heart as you do looking in the mirror? There's nothing wrong with working out or being well-groomed - unless there's nothing inside. Most of us struggle with something about our physical appearance, but it really doesn't matter to God! He made you the way you are.

That day all Jesse's sons were presented, but the future king wasn't among them. It was the youngest one, tending the sheep, whom God had chosen. How many times does God ignore our choice and go for the one everyone's written off? As it turned out, David was good-looking too.

So he sent for him and had him brought in. He was glowing with health and had a fine appearance and handsome features.

Then the Lord said, "Rise and anoint him; this is the one." So Samuel took the horn of oil and anointed him in the presence of his brothers, and from that day on the Spirit of the Lord came powerfully upon David. Samuel then went to Ramah. (12-13)

David's life was about to change. David needed the Spirit's anointing for the power to serve God, just as Saul had and the disciples in Acts would. You need that same anointing. We've already seen the Spirit poured out several times in this book. Has he come powerfully upon you?

David ends up in Saul's palace

God has a great sense of humor, arranging for Saul to actually invite his successor into his home!

Now the Spirit of the Lord had departed from Saul, and an evil spirit from the Lord tormented him.

Saul's attendants said to him, "See, an evil spirit from God is tormenting you. Let our lord command his servants here to search for someone who can play the lyre. He will play when the evil spirit from God comes on you, and you will feel better."

So Saul said to his attendants, "Find someone who plays well and bring him to me."

One of the servants answered, "I have seen a son of Jesse of Bethlehem who knows how to play the lyre. He is a brave man and a warrior. He speaks well and is a fine-looking man. And the Lord is with him."

Then Saul sent messengers to Jesse and said, "Send me your son David, who is with the sheep." So Jesse took a donkey loaded with bread, a skin of wine and a young goat and sent them with his son David to Saul.

David came to Saul and entered his service. Saul liked him very much, and David became one of his armor-bearers. Then Saul sent word to Jesse, saying, "Allow David to remain in my service, for I am pleased with him."

Whenever the spirit from God came on Saul, David would take up his lyre and play. Then relief would come to Saul; he would feel better, and the evil spirit would leave him. (14-23)

As can happen when a relationship ends up going sour, things started out great between Saul and David. Saul had never heard of him, but it just so happens his servant knew about this good looking kid who plays the lyre, speaks well, and is a brave man and warrior. He had everything Saul lacked, which drew Saul to him - but also spawned intense jealousy. Most important, God was with him. We can quench and grieve the Spirit so he effectively leaves us, and Saul's disobedience had led to the Spirit's departure.

An evil spirit from God?

More sobering is what can come in his place. When you're in rebellion and without the Holy Spirit you're open to evil spirits. But is God in the business of sending demons? Isn't that Satan's work?

It's not the only time in Scripture an evil spirit comes from God.[43] God is sovereign. If we focus too much on the devil we may think this is a great contest of equals, but Satan does only what he's allowed. God could immediately and completely bind him and all his demons, but he uses them to accomplish his purposes, which in this case was to get David into the king's palace.

The Jewish historian Josephus wrote in the first century: "But as for Saul, some strange and demonical disorders came upon him, and brought upon him such suffocations as were ready to choke him." His torment wasn't constant, but whatever form it took, it was obvious to those around him. Don't get hung up on whether a Christian can be demon possessed. New Testament Greek speaks of being "demonized," not "possessed" by a demon. When believers repeatedly give in to temptation and live in sin they will be tormented and oppressed by evil spirits, and in time Satan begins to build a stronghold.

Relief from the torment

God sent the evil spirit to Saul; then used the worship music of his newly anointed successor to bring him relief! What was it about David's playing that was so effective? A skilled musician who didn't know God could have played the same lyre to no effect. There's no magical power in music, but Spirit-filled believers who exalt God in worship send evil spirits fleeing. Far more than a way to feel good in church, worship is a powerful means of defeating the enemy and drawing close to God. Expect the devil to fight back:

The next day an evil spirit from God came forcefully on Saul. He was prophesying in his house, while David was playing the lyre, as he usually did. Saul had a spear in his hand and he hurled it, saying to himself, "I'll pin David to the wall." But David eluded him twice. (18:10-11, cf. 19:9-10)

What's puzzling is that Saul was "prophesying" after the evil spirit came on him, and in the midst of that he attempted to murder God's anointed! He'd previously prophesied when God's Spirit came on him, in the company of the prophets. Perhaps the evil spirit mimicked what the Holy Spirit had earlier inspired. It doesn't invalidate Saul's prior experience, but it does reveal an intense inner struggle, and the danger of entering the supernatural realm when your heart's not right with God.

People in sin and demonically oppressed often find comfort in Christian music, reading the Bible, or attending church, but if there's no genuine repentance the comfort will be temporary. Saul never repented. He found relief, but it didn't last. Instead, he became obsessed with killing the very one who helped him.

Are you in this chapter?

Are you a Saul? Has God's Spirit departed because of your repeated sin? Are you continuing the charade as a Christian or minister long after the power is gone? Are you tormented by evil spirits or obsessed with jealousy over another man God is using? Humble yourself, repent with your whole heart, and dedicate yourself anew to following Jesus. Fill your life with worship to God. Seek out a Spirit-filled brother to minister to you. When you get your life right with Jesus, those spirits will flee.

Are you a Samuel? Perhaps God has mightily used you, but you're older now, and feel your time is past. Are you still grieving over someone who turned away from the Lord, perhaps feeling that somehow you were responsible? Is God telling you to move on and let go of him? God needs your wisdom and maturity in raising up new leaders, even if your role is less active.

Or are you a David? You've gotten a word that God has great things for you, but you're working under someone who's jealous and tries to sabotage everything you do. Seeing his sin, you're tempted to undermine him, or leave. God may have you there for a purpose. He may be preparing you in that furnace, testing your trust in him for the right timing and your willingness to honor someone in authority. Let God remove that person. Don't try to manipulate the situation. If you have a chance to minister to him, do so. Remember, you're not wrestling with flesh and blood. Be alert to the spiritual dimensions of the battle, and stay in worship and fellowship with God. Above all, stay humble. Learn from the mistakes you've witnessed, and realize you're who you are by God's grace.

If you stay on Saul's path, you're headed for disaster. God has great plans for you, even though it's not possible for all of us to be a David. Part of maturity is accepting, flourishing, and being faithful wherever God has called you.

Chapter 14

Making the Most of the Rest of Your Life: 1 Samuel 17- 26

A
s you get older, it's harder to escape the consequences of
your earlier decisions. You really do reap what you sow. In
Saul's case, that meant life would be hard, since he'd
made some bad choices. Yet, by God's grace, there was still hope
for him if he was willing to humble himself and make some
changes.

Put your fear aside and encourage a younger man in his faith

Chapter 17 really belongs in a book on David. He's the hero,
while Saul looks pathetic. It's the same old routine. Saul and his
men assemble to face the Philistines and their new "secret
weapon," the giant Goliath, who comes out every day to
challenge Israel.

*On hearing the Philistine's words, Saul and all the Israelites were
dismayed and terrified.* (17:11)

Be careful who you listen to. Saul wasn't listening to God. All he
could hear were Goliath's taunts. Men follow their leader, and
Saul's fear and cowardice infect the entire army. Israel would
have faced certain defeat if God hadn't sent a giant killer, a
young man with a heart after God. *David said to Saul, "Let no
one lose heart on account of this Philistine; your servant will go*

and fight him." Saul replied, "You are not able to go out against this Philistine and fight him; you are only a boy, and he has been a fighting man from his youth." (17:32-33)

The unbelieving heart says "you can't" - and the facts often seem to confirm that. Faith doesn't ignore the facts. It faces them – but comes to a different conclusion. A young man weaker than David might get discouraged and give up at this point. If you have a Saul who is unrelentingly negative, don't give up. Tell him what God has done and stand strong for his honor, unmoved from what he's placed in your heart. *But David said to Saul, "Your servant has been keeping his father's sheep. When a lion or a bear came and carried off a sheep from the flock, I went after it, struck it and rescued the sheep from its mouth. When it turned on me, I seized it by its hair, struck it and killed it. Your servant has killed both the lion and the bear; this uncircumcised Philistine will be like one of them, because he has defied the armies of the living God. The Lord who delivered me from the paw of the lion and the paw of the bear will deliver me from the hand of this Philistine."* (17:34-36)

David strengthened his faith by applying what he learned in lesser battles. God loves childlike faith. Rejoice in it and offer guidance, but don't undermine it with your fears. It was humbling, but at least Saul encourages him: *Saul said to David, "Go, and the Lord be with you."* (17:34-37)

Better late than never. You may have experienced some rough times and become cynical. You're not up to fighting giants anymore, and that's okay. Do what you can to encourage the faith of young giant killers. We need them. We don't want to discourage them. If their heart's in the right place, God will use them as surely as he used David.

Don't weigh a young man down with your baggage

Then Saul dressed David in his own tunic. He put a coat of armor on him and a bronze helmet on his head. David fastened on his sword over the tunic and tried walking around, because he was not used to them.

"I cannot go in these," he said to Saul, "because I am not used to them." So he took them off. (17:38-39)

It was very symbolic and unexpectedly considerate, but what fit Saul doesn't fit David. It's too heavy. He's not used to fighting with all that. Older, well-meaning leaders may try to load you down with their stuff. It may look good and feel good to put on the king's tunic. The world values it, but God doesn't. It will only slow you down. Instead of adding more weight, get rid of the excess baggage and trust in the Lord. David's wise enough to take it off, proving you don't need the world's armor. When you're past your fighting years, you can have a great ministry equipping younger warriors. You have much to offer them, but be careful of weighing them down with things that aren't of God.

We all know what happened with Goliath. It was a game changer. With the giant's death, David becomes a national hero. It was one more defeat for Saul, who was still king, and should have been the one to kill Goliath.

Beware of jealousy

Whatever Saul sent him to do, David did it so successfully that Saul gave him a high rank in the army. This pleased all the people, and Saul's officers as well.

When the men were returning home after David had killed the Philistine, the women came out from all the towns of Israel to meet King Saul with singing and dancing, with joyful songs and with tambourines and lutes. As they danced, they sang:

"Saul has slain his thousands,
and David his tens of thousands."

Saul was very angry; this refrain galled him. "They have credited David with tens of thousands," he thought, "but me with only thousands. What more can he get but the kingdom?" And from that time on Saul kept a jealous eye on David. (18:5-9)

It's bad enough to lose God's anointing, and even worse to be shown up by a young kid, but Saul needed David. He'd saved Israel and was the only one who brought Saul relief from evil spirits. It's hard to crucify your pride, take the lower place, and acknowledge that someone else might be better. You can make way for him and rejoice that God will be glorified and your church will thrive, or you can get jealous and try to destroy him. Not surprisingly, Saul succumbed to jealousy, and it consumed him. Are you jealous of someone who seems to have greater success and anointing? Envious of their youth, good looks, and gifts?

Jealousy gives way to fear. The people loved David, but Saul feared him. Perhaps unwittingly, Saul put David in a position where he could further distinguish himself. When God is with someone, they'll be successful in whatever they do.

Saul was afraid of David, because the Lord was with David but had departed from Saul. So he sent David away from him and gave him command over a thousand men, and David led the troops in their campaigns. In everything he did he had great success, because the Lord was with him. When Saul saw how successful he was, he was afraid of him. But all Israel and Judah loved David, because he led them in their campaigns. (18:12-16)

Join the prophets

Somehow, in the midst of his sin and unbelief, Saul had one more dramatic encounter with the Spirit of God. The situation's bizarre. Saul's pursuit of David leads him right into the midst of a school of prophets. Apparently David and Samuel had gone there to spend some time prophesying, worshiping the Lord, and getting filled with the Spirit. It's the last time the three are together.

When David had fled and made his escape, he went to Samuel at Ramah and told him all that Saul had done to him. Then he and Samuel went to Naioth and stayed there. Word came to Saul: "David is in Naioth at Ramah"; so he sent men to capture him. But when they saw a group of prophets prophesying, with Samuel standing there as their leader, the Spirit of God came upon Saul's men and they also prophesied. Saul was told about it, and he sent more men, and they prophesied too. Saul sent men a third time, and they also prophesied. Finally, he himself left for Ramah and went to the great cistern at Secu. And he asked, "Where are Samuel and David?"

"Over in Naioth at Ramah," they said.

So Saul went to Naioth at Ramah. But the Spirit of God came even on him, and he walked along prophesying until he came to Naioth. He stripped off his garments, and he too prophesied in Samuel's presence. He lay naked all that day and all that night. This is why people say, "Is Saul also among the prophets?" (19:18-24)

What if Saul had given up pursuing David, handed him the kingdom, and spent the rest of his life in the Lord's presence with the prophets? Was God mercifully giving him one more chance?

Do we need a Naoith at Ramah today?

Wouldn't it be great if the Spirit's presence was as strong in our churches? Can you imagine people coming in and falling under the Spirit's power, prophesying and speaking in tongues? If God could touch Saul, he can touch anyone! He was lying there naked all day and night. We don't need anyone naked, but could we give the Spirit that freedom?

How about a refuge like Naioth at Ramah, to meet God and his prophets? A place of renewal for someone fleeing their home, so anointed that murderers seeking a man's life would fall under God's power.

A place for hurting men like David - a safe place when you're pursued by the enemy. A place of twenty-four-hour worship, where you can hear the voice of the Spirit in the company of prophets.

Don't kill the men of God

In the midst of the prophesying David escapes and Saul temporarily gives up pursuit. But instead of nurturing what God did, he allows his fear and jealousy to take over. Clearly satanically inspired, he commits his worst deed yet.

Then the king sent for the priest Ahimelech son of Ahitub and his father's whole family, who were the priests at Nob, and they all came to the king. Saul said, "Listen now, son of Ahitub."

"Yes, my lord," he answered.

Saul said to him, "Why have you conspired against me, you and the son of Jesse, giving him bread and a sword and inquiring of God for him, so that he has rebelled against me and lies in wait for me, as he does today?"

Ahimelech answered the king, "Who of all your servants is as loyal as David, the king's son-in-law, captain of your bodyguard and highly respected in your household? Was that day the first time I inquired of God for him? Of course not! Let not the king accuse your servant or any of his father's family, for your servant knows nothing at all about this whole affair." (22:11-15)

God's giving Saul an out. The man of God is speaking common sense, the truth, but Saul's thinking is twisted by the devil's lies and deceit. He could have humbled himself, thanked the priest for helping his son-in-law, and spared himself further judgment.

But with a heart hardened by sin and envy, he has no fear of God or respect for his servants.

But the king said, "You will surely die, Ahimelech, you and your father's whole family."

Then the king ordered the guards at his side: "Turn and kill the priests of the Lord, because they too have sided with David. They knew he was fleeing, yet they did not tell me." But the king's officials were not willing to raise a hand to strike the priests of the Lord.

The king then ordered Doeg, "You turn and strike down the priests." So Doeg the Edomite turned and struck them down. That day he killed eighty-five men who wore the linen ephod. He also put to the sword Nob, the town of the priests, with its men and women, its children and infants, and its cattle, donkeys and sheep. (22:16-19)

It took a gentile Edomite to kill the priests. No Jew would do it. When God commanded Saul to totally destroy Amelech, he disobeyed. Now he doesn't hesitate to destroy everything, yet he accomplished nothing. David's still out there, and Saul has further alienated himself from the Lord.

Responding to injustice

Saul wasn't as clueless as he might look. Broken and hardened, bound up and unable to change, he was still capable of tenderness toward David. David seemed to delight in surprising Saul, and on more than one occasion could have killed him.

When David finished saying this, Saul asked, "Is that your voice, David my son?" And he wept aloud. "You are more righteous than I," he said. "You have treated me well, but I have treated you badly. You have just now told me about the good you did to me; the Lord delivered me into your hands, but you did not kill me. When a man finds his enemy, does he let him get away unharmed? May the Lord reward you well for the way you treated me today. I know that you will surely be king and that the kingdom of Israel will be established in your hands. Now swear to me by the Lord that you will not kill off my descendants or wipe out my name from my father's family."

So David gave his oath to Saul. Then Saul returned home, but David and his men went up to the stronghold. (24:16-22)

No one would have blamed David for killing Saul. No one had to know. Yet centuries before Jesus taught us to love our enemies, David had a heart that was right with God. He consistently honored his elders and those in authority, refusing to touch the king's anointed. He didn't take things into his own hands, but trusted God to deal with Saul. He was also wise enough not to stay around and be abused. He returned with his men to the stronghold, and let Saul self-destruct.

Saul could have given it up here. But, like most men, his pride wouldn't let him, so he kept up the pursuit. He never thought to humble himself, repent, and seek the Lord. He might have saved his life and enjoyed his later years if he'd handed the kingdom over to his God-chosen successor. After all, David was already in the family.

If you find yourself in a situation like David's:

- Maintain your honor and do the right thing, even when you see tremendous corruption in those over you.

- Resist the temptation to undermine them – but do what you can to avoid the worst of their poison.

- Pray for them. You can pray in faith for the "mountain" to be removed into the sea, but be aware it may not move. God often has purposes in allowing the mountain to remain.

- Don't even think of murder. Seriously!

- Try to redirect them from pointless battles to the real enemy.

- You may actually be able to minister to them, like David playing the lyre for Saul. It can be hard and feel awkward, but allow God to use you.

Make the most of the rest of your life

God wants you to learn from your mistakes and gently mentor young men so they can avoid them. I meet many men crushed by disappointment and failure. If we're not careful, those burdens can become debilitating. There's something very refreshing about seeing a young man on fire for Jesus, full of faith and energy to serve the King of kings. Don't withdraw, get cynical, or discourage their passion.

You've probably had disappointments. Instead of living in the past with your regrets, you can make the most of what you have.

- Accept the death of some dreams. It's okay to mourn them.

- Humble yourself and acknowledge your share of the responsibility for what's happened in your life.

- Stop playing the blame game and make the most of the time you have left.

God will give you viable alternatives. There were a number of things Saul could have done:

- Invest in his son-in-law and successor. He could have influenced and supported David, while growing himself.

- He had an impressive son. He could have gotten to know Jonathan and spent time with him.

- It certainly wouldn't have hurt him to spend time with the prophets. People had already asked "Is Saul among the prophets?" He could have had a third career in the school of the prophets!

- Spend time with his two daughters, learning to be a grandfather.

- He'd had his victories. He could take a careful look at what had worked in his life and try to reconnect with the Lord, nurturing what God had done in the past.

Even though Saul lost his earthly kingdom, he could have used his remaining years preparing for the coming kingdom, while helping others develop their kingly authority. Despite his failures, Saul had some good options. He still had a lot going for him, and you do too. Resist the bitterness and negativity. God wants you to make the most of the rest of your life.

Chapter 15

Saul the Family Man:
1 Samuel 18, 19, 20, 23

I t's not surprising that a chapter on Saul's family comes almost at the end of his story. A man's family often takes a back seat to his pursuit of fame and fortune. It's only when life starts slowing down that he may wake up and long for relationships he never took the time to develop. In his retirement Saul could have spent time with his family, making up for all those years he was gone fighting battles and chasing David. It wouldn't have been easy. Jonathan probably didn't feel too great about his dad's obsession with killing his best friend, or almost dying for eating that honey. Sometimes it's easier to fight the Philistines than deal with matters of the heart in your own home, but hopefully by this point a man has the strength and depth of character to lovingly persist, putting himself aside and bearing the anger and resentment he may have been responsible for. On their death bed no man regrets not spending more time or energy on his job. His regrets center around his family. Don't wait until you're dying to make things right.

At home the real man is on display. Our personal issues usually are much more evident there. You aren't one flesh with anyone on your job, unless you work with your wife! Your success loving a woman (and I'm not talking about sex) validates your masculinity as much as your great exploits in the world. Your relationship with her touches your core – and too often what it touches is shame, failure, and incompetence. Father/son relationships also tend to be emotionally intense. Many men spend a lifetime longing for the father who was never there, angry about his failures. And even though we love our children, we frequently feel conflicted and guilty about our relationships with them. Capable men with successful ministries and careers can be terrible husbands and fathers. Yet family is important to God. An elder must have children who *believe and are not open to the charge of being wild and disobedient.*[44] *He must manage his own family well and see that his children obey him with proper respect. (If anyone does not know how to manage his own family, how can he take care of God's church?)*[45]

We don't know anything about Saul's father or their relationship, and very little about his family. Chances are if Saul's public life was a disaster, his home life was worse. Though certainly a worthy investment for his latter years, dedicating his time to the family might not have been easy or appealing for Saul.

What we know about Saul's family

- Saul married Ahinoam, and they had four sons (Jonathan, Abinadab, Malchisua or Malki-Shua, and Ish-Bosheth or Esh-Baal) and two daughters (Merab and Michal).

- We know nothing else about Abinadab and Malchisua, except they died along with Jonathan and their father in that final battle, casualties of Saul's insecurities and failures.

- Ish-Bosheth was the only survivor - and the legitimate heir to the throne - after Saul's death. With the help of his uncle Abner he ruled for about two years, until David established his reign over the entire nation. Two of his own captains beheaded Ish-Bosheth in his bed.

- Saul also had two sons, Armoni and Mephibosheth, with a concubine named Rizpah. Unlike David, there's no other record of any womanizing.

- David delivered Rizpah's two sons, along with Merab's five sons (Saul's grandsons) to the Gibeonites, as compensation for what Saul had done to that nation. They were all killed.[46]

- Jonathan had one son, Mephibosheth (named after his uncle, also called Merib-Baal), who was five when his father died. Because of his covenant with Jonathan, David cared for him until his death.

- He had one son, Micah, of whom we know nothing except for numerous descendants listed in I Chronicles 8.

Saul never had the chance to enjoy his family in retirement. We have to read between the lines to learn what kind of father he was.

Jonathan and David

Somehow Saul produced an exceptional son who should have been king, and probably would have been a good one. He was a courageous man, full of life and the Spirit, who'd already shown himself superior to his dad. He had a fiercely loyal armor bearer. He was a kindred spirit with David, and made a covenant with him. Instead of resenting David for inheriting a throne that should have been his, he graciously accepted his fate and embraced him.

After David had finished talking with Saul, Jonathan became one in spirit with David, and he loved him as himself. From that day Saul kept David with him and did not let him return home to his family. And Jonathan made a covenant with David because he loved him as himself. Jonathan took off the robe he was wearing and gave it to David, along with his tunic, and even his sword, his bow and his belt. (18:1-4)

Giving David these personal items was a powerful expression of love, as well as an acknowledgment that David would need that robe as the next king. Later, he helped David flee from Saul.

So Jonathan made a covenant with the house of David, saying, "May the Lord call David's enemies to account." And Jonathan had David reaffirm his oath out of love for him, because he loved him as he loved himself.

After the boy had gone, David got up from the south side of the stone and bowed down before Jonathan three times, with his face to the ground. Then they kissed each other and wept together—but David wept the most.

Jonathan said to David, "Go in peace, for we have sworn friendship with each other in the name of the Lord, saying, 'The Lord is witness between you and me, and between your descendants and my descendants forever.'" Then David left, and Jonathan went back to the town. (20: 16, 17, 41-42)

There's a depth of male friendship which many men never know. Would you feel comfortable being that close to another man? Have you ever had such a friendship? Most men long for it - but also fear it. Today, a man who talks about loving another man is immediately suspected of being gay. Hugs have become common, but most men are still uncomfortable with too much physical contact, and some struggle with underlying fears of possibly being gay. Yet one of the best ways to deal with same-sex attraction is to have close, healthy, non-sexual relationships with other men.

There appears to be just one more time Jonathan saw David, while Saul was pursuing him:

While David was at Horesh in the Desert of Ziph, he learned that Saul had come out to take his life. And Saul's son Jonathan went to David at Horesh and helped him find strength in God. "Don't be afraid," he said. "My father Saul will not lay a hand on you. You will be king over Israel, and I will be second to you. Even my father Saul knows this." The two of them made a covenant before the Lord. Then Jonathan went home, but David remained at Horesh. (23:15-18)

What a beautiful example of God's intent for friendship! Jonathan sought David out at one of the most difficult times in his life. They renewed their covenant, and Jonathan encouraged David in his calling. Most important, he helped David find strength in God. When the enemy's in pursuit, the strength you need can only be found in the Lord. Do you have someone who will seek you out and pray with you at the toughest times? Is there someone you can minister to in that way?

Saul's daughters

Saul said to David, "Here is my older daughter Merab. I will give her to you in marriage; only serve me bravely and fight the battles of the Lord." For Saul said to himself, "I will not raise a hand against him. Let the Philistines do that!"

But David said to Saul, "Who am I, and what is my family or my father's clan in Israel, that I should become the king's son-in-law?" So when the time came for Merab, Saul's daughter, to be given to David, she was given in marriage to Adriel of Meholah. (18:17-19)

Saul doesn't show much regard for his daughter, using her as a pawn for his own purposes. Instead of blessing her, he's hoping to kill her future husband. David refused the king's offer, either because God showed him Saul's wicked intent, he was being humble, or he already had his eye on her younger sister. As Saul's luck would have it, that sister was in love with David. Saul can't escape people's attraction to him! But again he sees an opportunity to get David killed, even if it breaks his daughter's heart:

Now Saul's daughter Michal was in love with David, and when they told Saul about it, he was pleased. "I will give her to him," he thought, "so that she may be a snare to him and so that the hand of the Philistines may be against him." So Saul said to David, "Now you have a second opportunity to become my son-in-law."

Then Saul ordered his attendants: "Speak to David privately and say, 'Look, the king is pleased with you, and his attendants all like you; now become his son-in-law.'"

They repeated these words to David. But David said, "Do you think it is a small matter to become the king's son-in-law? I'm only a poor man and little known."

When Saul's servants told him what David had said, Saul replied, "Say to David, 'The king wants no other price for the bride than a hundred Philistine foreskins, to take revenge on his enemies.'" Saul's plan was to have David fall by the hands of the Philistines.

When the attendants told David these things, he was pleased to become the king's son-in-law. So before the allotted time elapsed, David and his men went out and killed two hundred Philistines. He brought their foreskins and presented the full number to the king so that he might become the king's son-in-law. Then Saul gave him his daughter Michal in marriage. (18:20-27)

Maybe it was the custom – but what kind of man wants a collection of a hundred foreskins? And what kind of man complies? A man in love! And a young, daring, man who likes the challenge. Picturing David satisfying Saul's requirement is pretty ugly, but, extreme as it was, David happily did it, and Saul had no choice but to give him his daughter.

When Saul realized that the Lord was with David and that his daughter Michal loved David, Saul became still more afraid of him, and he remained his enemy the rest of his days.

The Philistine commanders continued to go out to battle, and as often as they did, David met with more success than the rest of Saul's officers, and his name became well known. (18:28-30)

God may have arranged the marriage to Michal to protect his anointed, since she ended up saving David's life.

Saul sent men to David's house to watch it and to kill him in the morning. But Michal, David's wife, warned him, "If you don't run for your life tonight, tomorrow you'll be killed." So Michal let David down through a window, and he fled and escaped. Then Michal took an idol and laid it on the bed, covering it with a garment and putting some goats' hair at the head.

When Saul sent the men to capture David, Michal said, "He is ill."

Then Saul sent the men back to see David and told them, "Bring him up to me in his bed so that I may kill him." But when the men entered, there was the idol in the bed, and at the head was some goats' hair.

Saul said to Michal, "Why did you deceive me like this and send my enemy away so that he escaped?"

Michal told him, "He said to me, 'Let me get away. Why should I kill you?'" (19:11-17)

Being Saul's daughter couldn't have been easy. Any leader's children have it hard, but Michal really had it rough. She was the king's daughter and the wife of the future king, who also happened to be her father's chief rival. David kept her father half sane with his music, but was constantly in danger of his life. Women seem to suffer more from family conflict, and chances are Michal wasn't prepared for this challenge. She ended up following her father's path of lies, deception, and idolatry, deceiving Saul and then covering herself by giving her husband up to him.

As if all that didn't make it hard enough for her to establish a home, somehow Saul managed to take her away from David: *But Saul had given his daughter Michal, David's wife, to Paltiel son of Laish, who was from Gallim.* (25:44) After Saul's death David demanded that Ish-Bosheth give her back: *Then David sent messengers to Ish-Bosheth son of Saul, demanding, "Give me my wife Michal, whom I betrothed to myself for the price of a hundred Philistine foreskins."*

So Ish-Bosheth gave orders and had her taken away from her husband Paltiel son of Laish. Her husband, however, went with her, weeping behind her all the way to Bahurim. Then Abner said to him, "Go back home!" So he went back. (2 Samuel 3:14-16)

Michal was the first of David's many wives and concubines. She should have been the mother of the next king – even in the line of the Messiah. But not surprisingly, all these events sapped her love for David and made her bitter. Like her father, she ends her life alone.

As the ark of the Lord was entering the City of David, Michal daughter of Saul watched from a window. And when she saw King David leaping and dancing before the Lord, she despised him in her heart.

When David returned home to bless his household, Michal daughter of Saul came out to meet him and said, "How the king of Israel has distinguished himself today, disrobing in the sight of the slave girls of his servants as any vulgar fellow would!"

David said to Michal, "It was before the Lord, who chose me rather than your father or anyone from his house when he appointed me ruler over the Lord's people Israel—I will celebrate before the Lord. I will become even more undignified than this, and I will be humiliated in my own eyes. But by these slave girls you spoke of, I will be held in honor."

And Michal daughter of Saul had no children to the day of her death. (2 Samuel 6:16, 20-23)

Sad. I don't think there was much happiness in that household. In fact, David's family life in general was tragic. Saul's palace certainly had not provided a great model.

Families often get left behind in men's quest for greatness. Father, don't wait for life to slow down to enjoy your family. You leave a lasting impact on your children. If you're fortunate enough to have a son as outstanding as Jonathan, don't be jealous of him. Rejoice in his virility and encourage him. Don't sabotage your children's dreams or marriages, and don't take them to the grave with you.

Chapter 16

When Your Worst Fear Becomes Reality: 1 Samuel 28

esus said *"Enter through the narrow gate. For wide is the gate and broad is the road that leads to destruction, and many enter through it. But small is the gate and narrow the road that leads to life, and only a few find it."*[47] God called Saul to walk the narrow road. He equipped him to lead others on that road, building a nation that would glorify him. Kingly authority is found only on the narrow road. Yet, like all of us, Saul struggled with the attraction of the broad road and the restrictions of the narrow one. God kept calling him back to the narrow way, but Saul kept making decisions that placed him squarely on the road to destruction. He's finding it's not as attractive as it looks, but he's been deceived into thinking he can't go back. Faith-destroying fear dominates his life and keeps him from God, and now his worst fears are becoming reality.

Which road are you on? God's calling you to pass through the small gate and walk the narrow road with him. He'll give you the grace to do it. Don't listen to the lie that it's too late or you just can't make it on the narrow road. God commands you: Fear not! There will be battles ahead. It's not easy. But it's far better than the road to destruction.

Another battle with the Philistines

All his life Saul had fought the Philistines. He'd had some amazing victories, but things are different now. His mentor's dead. God has left him. Saul is alone.

Now Samuel was dead, and all Israel had mourned for him and buried him in his own town of Ramah. Saul had expelled the mediums and spiritists from the land. The Philistines assembled and came and set up camp at Shunem, while Saul gathered all the Israelites and set up camp at Gilboa. When Saul saw the Philistine army, he was afraid; terror filled his heart. (3-5)

Saul's tired of the battle. He goes through the motions, gathering the troops and setting up camp, but his heart isn't in it. In fact, it's filled with terror – intense, sharp, overwhelming fear. Has terror ever filled your heart? What are you afraid of right now? Is there an enemy you've fought all your life? Does it feel like he's about to destroy you? You may be tired of the battle, but don't give up. Don't give in, and don't be afraid. You may fight that enemy the rest of your life. Remember, if you want to be strong you've got to be tested. God allowed the Philistine attacks to demonstrate his power and glory, and keep Israel relying on him. When they looked to God, he always gave them victory.

What are you looking at?

Saul's problem started with his eyes. One look at the Philistine army and fear filled his heart. Just like Peter sank when he took his eyes off Jesus on that stormy sea, Saul is looking at the circumstances. God's nowhere to be seen. Our eyes often get us in trouble. Things are not always as they seem. Remember Elisha and his servant when enemies surrounded them?

When the servant of the man of God got up and went out early the next morning, an army with horses and chariots had surrounded the city. "Oh, my lord, what shall we do?" the servant asked. "Don't be afraid," the prophet answered. "Those who are with us are more than those who are with them." And Elisha prayed, "O Lord, open his eyes so he may see." Then the Lord opened the servant's eyes, and he looked and saw the hills full of horses and chariots of fire all around Elisha. [48]

Saul didn't have eyes of faith. Do you? What are you looking at? When fear fills your heart, wake up! You're probably looking at the wrong thing. Keep your eyes on Jesus.

When God is silent

He inquired of the Lord, but the Lord did not answer him by dreams or Urim or prophets. (6)

Saul did the right thing - but there was no response. No dream. No guidance from the Urim and Thummin - the sacred lots or stones Old Testament priests would throw like dice to discern God's will. Saul had killed many priests and probably alienated the rest. Samuel was dead. There may have been no prophet to speak. Saul only came to God when he needed something, and now God had turned away from him. Silence.

Have you ever needed to hear from God, but nothing works? You fast, search the Bible, and call trusted counselors, but come up empty. In desperation you may consider things you normally wouldn't, like turning to the devil. I've seen people call in spiritists when they pray for healing and there's no miracle. Saul knew mediums and spiritists were evil – he'd expelled them from the land. But he also knew they could contact the spirit world.

When you cast something out of your life, don't go back to it. Don't keep track of where the spiritists are – just in case you need one. I've known men who trash their pornography – but hide a few DVDs or magazines, just in case. Don't turn to Satan just because it seems like God isn't coming through for you.

Saul consults a medium

Saul then said to his attendants, "Find me a woman who is a medium, so I may go and inquire of her." "There is one in Endor," they said. So Saul disguised himself, putting on other clothes, and at night he and two men went to the woman.

"Consult a spirit for me," he said, "and bring up for me the one I name."

But the woman said to him, "Surely you know what Saul has done. He has cut off the mediums and spiritists from the land. Why have you set a trap for my life to bring about my death?"

Saul swore to her by the Lord, "As surely as the Lord lives, you will not be punished for this." (7-10)

You know what you're doing is wrong when you're in the devil's territory and don't want anyone to know. You find yourself sneaking around at night, putting on some kind of disguise, having to hide and cover yourself. You usually take others with you. Not only is Saul sinning, he took two men with him, and is making the woman break his own law. You may feel pressured to make oaths. When you swear by the Lord to cover your sin you're really in trouble. Never play with the devil. Don't even think about any contact with spiritists, mediums, witches – or anything remotely satanic. Renounce any fascination you might have with "the dark side."

A word from Samuel

Then the woman asked, "Whom shall I bring up for you?" "Bring up Samuel," he said.

When the woman saw Samuel, she cried out at the top of her voice and said to Saul, "Why have you deceived me? You are Saul!"

The king said to her, "Don't be afraid. What do you see?"
The woman said, "I see a ghostly figure coming up out of the earth."

"What does he look like?" he asked.

"An old man wearing a robe is coming up," she said.
Then Saul knew it was Samuel, and he bowed down and prostrated himself with his face to the ground. (11-14)

Her description of Samuel sounded right to Saul. He was even wearing his robe - perhaps the same robe Saul had grabbed and ripped.[49] Can mediums call up the dead? Scripture doesn't deny the reality of the spirit world. It just forbids contact with it. Was it really Samuel, and if so, why God would allow it? It may have been a satanic imposter to further terrorize Saul, even prophesying a lie to seal his fate. Or God may have allowed Samuel to appear to give him a final warning. That doesn't mean it was right to seek him, or that we should expect God to do the same for us.

When she saw Samuel she realized Saul had deceived her, and screamed, fearing for her life. Saul is deceived and is a deceiver just like Satan, the father of lies. When you're in sin, afraid, and far from God, you're wide open to deception. Watch out for it.

Samuel said to Saul, "Why have you disturbed me by bringing me up?"

"I am in great distress," Saul said. "The Philistines are fighting against me, and God has departed from me. He no longer answers me, either by prophets or by dreams. So I have called on you to tell me what to do." (15)

How sad. After all those years as king Saul still didn't have the strength to act on his own. He sounds like a little kid, dependent on others for survival. "I need someone to tell me what to do."

True, he asked God, and God didn't speak. But when God was talking, Saul didn't obey him.

If you find yourself in a desperate situation and have a godly mentor, by all means call on him. Unfortunately Samuel's dead, and Saul never developed his own relationship with God. Don't let a mentor take God's place. Don't run from person to person to get a word. Have some direction about your life. Keep the communication with God open. He'll give you godly counsel, but he also wants you to grow up.

As usual, Saul's caught up in his feelings:

- "I'm in great distress."

- "The Philistines are fighting against me."

- "God's turned away from me."

- "Life's tough."

- "Everything's falling apart."

- "I don't know what to do."

I've felt that way. I'm sure you have. David did too, but David came to God with an open, repentant, heart. He worked past his feelings to a renewed vision of God and his plans. Don't get sucked into a self-centered "woe is me" attitude. It will pull you further into despair.

Samuel said, "Why do you consult me, now that the Lord has departed from you and become your enemy? The Lord has done what he predicted through me. The Lord has torn the kingdom out of your hands and given it to one of your neighbors—to David. Because you did not obey the Lord or carry out his fierce wrath against the Amalekites, the Lord has done this to you today. The Lord will deliver both Israel and you into the hands of the Philistines, and tomorrow you and your sons will be with me.

The Lord will also give the army of Israel into the hands of the Philistines." (16-19)

As if Saul hadn't caused Samuel enough headaches in life, now he bothers him in the grave! While he was alive Samuel told Saul exactly what would happen. It's tragic when you're warned of the consequences but keep on doing the same thing. Saul's biggest nightmare is coming true, and there's nothing he can do about it. It's too late. By the next evening he and his sons will be dead, and Israel will be defeated.

Saul's last supper

Immediately Saul fell full length on the ground, filled with fear because of Samuel's words. His strength was gone, for he had eaten nothing all that day and all that night.

When the woman came to Saul and saw that he was greatly shaken, she said, "Look, your servant has obeyed you. I took my life in my hands and did what you told me to do. Now please listen to your servant and let me give you some food so you may eat and have the strength to go on your way."

He refused and said, "I will not eat." But his men joined the woman in urging him, and he listened to them. He got up from the ground and sat on the couch. The woman had a fattened calf at the house, which she butchered at once. She took some flour, kneaded it and baked bread without yeast. Then she set it before Saul and his men, and they ate. That same night they got up and left. (20-25)

How do you respond to bad news? It reveals what kind of man you are. You've probably seen movies of men facing death with great courage and dignity. Saul wasn't one of them. We can't blame him for being badly shaken and refusing to eat. With his strength gone and filled with fear, he falls out. He was a basket case. Fortunately the witch is more together than the king and takes care of him. It was his "last supper."

Satan may come knocking at your door. That old enemy who's haunted you all your life shows up again. The Philistines are back. Terror and desperation fill your heart. There seems to be no way out. God's silent. No one else seems to be there for you. Saul's reached the end of the broad road. The next day he'll commit suicide. The devil's out to destroy you and will stop at nothing. Don't let your life get to this point.

Chapter 17

The End:
1 Samuel 31

This is a hard chapter. You want to finish a book with something powerful, but we've been following Saul on his depressing decline for a while, and already know there'd be no happy ending. Saul was made to reign. God chose him and gave him everything he needed, and Saul squandered it. He never learned to use his authority. Because of his repeated disobedience God rejected him, withdrew his Holy Spirit, and sent evil spirits to oppress him. Now Saul's reached the end of the road. Not surprisingly, he ends his life in the most cowardly way possible.

Now the Philistines fought against Israel; the Israelites fled before them, and many fell dead on Mount Gilboa. (1)

When you're in a losing battle, don't keep fighting. Know when to surrender and get help. Saul should have done that long ago. Had he called on David he might have spared the nation defeat and avoided his own death, as well as his sons'.

The Philistines were in hot pursuit of Saul and his sons, and they killed his sons Jonathan, Abinadab and Malki-Shua. The fighting grew fierce around Saul, and when the archers overtook him, they wounded him critically. (2-3)

Can you feel the desperation? There's no turning back. Saul's looking death in the face, reaping what he's sown. He could go out valiantly, throwing himself on God's mercy in last-minute repentance to save his soul, but Saul's never been one to humble himself.

Saul said to his armor-bearer, "Draw your sword and run me through, or these uncircumcised fellows will come and run me through and abuse me."

But his armor-bearer was terrified and would not do it; so Saul took his own sword and fell on it. When the armor-bearer saw that Saul was dead, he too fell on his sword and died with him. So Saul and his three sons and his armor-bearer and all his men died together that same day. (4-6)

None of the options were good. Saul couldn't take the thought of being killed by the Philistines, so he chooses suicide - the ultimate act of desperation, and a cowardly end to a wasted life. He certainly isn't alone. I've had many men tell me they'd kill themselves before getting caught and facing more jail time. Or to spare their families more pain if they got caught up again in drugs or sexual sin. In a twisted way it makes sense. There's nothing wrong with you if you've contemplated suicide. The devil will try every temptation possible in his attempt to destroy you.

When the Israelites along the valley and those across the Jordan saw that the Israelite army had fled and that Saul and his sons had died, they abandoned their towns and fled. And the Philistines came and occupied them.

The next day, when the Philistines came to strip the dead, they found Saul and his three sons fallen on Mount Gilboa. They cut off his head and stripped off his armor, and they sent messengers throughout the land of the Philistines to proclaim the news in the temple of their idols and among their people. They put his armor

*in the temple of the Ashtoreths and fastened his body to the wall
of Beth Shan.*

*When the people of Jabesh Gilead heard what the Philistines had
done to Saul, all their valiant men marched through the night to
Beth Shan. They took down the bodies of Saul and his sons from
the wall of Beth Shan and went to Jabesh, where they burned
them. Then they took their bones and buried them under a
tamarisk tree at Jabesh, and they fasted seven days.* (7-13)

First Chronicles says Saul died because he was unfaithful to God.
He didn't keep the word of the Lord or inquire of God, *"so the
Lord put him to death."*[50] Saul's life reflects that mysterious
mixture of God's sovereign work and man's responsibility. God
chose, called, and equipped him with everything he needed to
reign. Saul lost his life and his kingdom because of poor choices.
He took his own life, but Chronicles says God put him to death.

In Daniel chapter four, God tells King Nebuchadnezzar: *"Your
royal authority has been taken away from you,"* yet he humbled
himself, repented, and acknowledged God. By the end of that
chapter his authority was restored. Saul lost his kingly authority,
but never repented. You too can lose that authority. You already
may have. But it's not too late for you to humble yourself,
repent, and seek the Lord for that authority to be restored.

Saul ended his own story, but unfortunately for him it's not
really the end of the story. Nobody has the power to truly end
their story. This life is just a dress rehearsal and training for
eternity. God's desire was for Saul to have a place in that eternal
kingdom. Instead, he will spend eternity separated from God in
torment. He'd tasted the ecstasy of worship to the living God
and the torment of evil spirits – and chose the latter.

God's story was just beginning. His work won't stop because of
one man's disobedience. Sure, there will be plenty of battles
along the way. Just as Adam, Eli, Samuel, and Saul disappointed

him, there will be many who fail to live up to their potential to exercise God's authority in his kingdom. Even David, the man after God's own heart, had serious failures. The history of the church is littered with sin and men abusing that authority. Satan is relentless in his determination to destroy God's kingdom and take the throne himself. But we know that something amazing happened at Calvary, when God's own Son paid the price for our sin, humbled himself to the point of death on a cross, and conclusively defeated the power of the evil one. His glorious resurrection and ascension to his Father's right hand to reign eternally are only the beginning of a kingdom of righteousness and peace. Whatever it takes, and however long it takes, God will have everyone he needs to share that reign and carry out the business of his kingdom. He wants you to have a part in it and take your rightful place, learning to exercise kingly authority now.

There may be things in Saul's life that remind you of yourself. Hopefully you haven't made the same bad decisions, but if you have, it's not too late to come back to the Lord and get things right. God wants to use everything that's happened to you so far to prepare you to reign with him eternally. Even though you've been marred by sin, you still bear God's kingly image. Use that authority for the good of your family and his kingdom. It's not an easy road, but you're not alone. Rise up and take your place as God's adopted son. You were made to reign!

Notes

1. Genesis 1:28

2. Judges 6:36-40; Judges 16

3. I Samuel 1

4. I Samuel 2:30-35

5. Zechariah 7:13

6. I Samuel 9:2

7. See Genesis 24:11-28, where Abraham's servant met Rebekah at the well, and John 4, where Jesus met the Samaritan woman.

8. See Judges 20:46-48

9. Revelation 1:6

10. Brian Doerksen and Steve Mitchinson, Copyright 2000 Vineyard Songs (UK/Eire). Used by permission.

11. Think of Joseph, in jail in the morning and second most important man in Egypt by evening (Genesis 41), or Jesus' move to ministry from the carpenter shop.

12. Watch for many insights into spiritual fathers and sons as we follow Samuel and Saul.

13. See I Samuel 3

14. Numbers 11:24-29

15. John 4:23

16. See Acts 2

17. See Joshua 1

18. Luke 11:13

19. Galatians 3:1-5

20. Larry Crabb wrote a great book on this, *The Silence of Adam*

21. See John Bevere's excellent book *The Fear of the Lord* for more on this.

22. Matthew 5:38-48

23. Romans 12:18-20

24. Joshua 4:19-24

25. I Samuel 10:7

26. John R. W. Stott, *Baptism & Fullness* (Downers Grove, IL: InterVarsity Press, 1976).

27. Dr. Phil McGraw wrote a good book on that called *Real Life: Preparing for the 7 Most Challenging Days of Your Life*.

28. Deuteronomy 7:2

29. II Corinthians 6:14-7:1

30. I Corinthians 7:12-16

31. II Corinthians 10:4

32. Ephesians 6:10-18

33. Joshua 1

34. Psalm 138

35. Proverbs 28:1

36. Proverbs 21:29

37. Jeremiah 32:17

38. Exodus 17:8-16

39. Psalm 6, 13, and 79, among others

40. Joshua 4

41. Matthew 7:21-23; 25:31-46

42. 2 Timothy 2:12

43. See Judges 9:23 and I Kings 22:20-22

44. Titus 1:6

45. I Timothy 3:4-5

46. II Samuel 21:8-9

47. Matthew 7:13-14

48. 2 Kings 6:15-17

49. I Samuel 15:27-28

50. I Chronicles 10:13-14